What You Can Do About SICKLE CELL DISEASE

CONTEMPORARY DISEASES AND DISORDERS

What You Can Do About SICKLE CELL DISEASE

Monique Vescia, Alvin and Virginia Silverstein, and Laura Silverstein Nunn

Enslow Publishing
101 W. 23rd Street
Suite 240
New York, NY 10011
USA
enslow.com

Published in 2016 by Enslow Publishing, LLC
101 W. 23rd Street, Suite 240, New York, NY 10011

Library of Congress Cataloging-in-Publication Data
Vescia, Monique.
What you can do about sickle cell disease / Monique Vescia, Alvin and Virginia Silverstein, and Laura Silverstein Nunn.
pages cm. — (Contemporary diseases and disorders)
Audience: Age 12-up.
Audience: Grade 7 to 8.
Summary: "Discusses the conditions of sickle cell disease, the latest research, and treatment options"—Provided by publisher.
Includes bibliographical references and index.
ISBN 978-0-7660-7040-0
1. Sickle cell anemia—Juvenile literature. I. Silverstein, Alvin. II. Silverstein, Virginia B. III. Nunn, Laura Silverstein. IV. Title.
RC641.7.S5V47 2016
616.1'527—dc23
2015015552

Printed in the United States of America

To Our Readers: We have done our best to make sure all Web site addresses in this book were active and appropriate when we went to press. However, the author and the publisher have no control over and assume no liability for the material available on those Web sites or on any Web sites they may link to. Any comments or suggestions can be sent by e-mail to customerservice@enslow.com.

Portions of this book originally appeared in the book *The Sickle Cell Anemia Update.*

Photo Credits: Anidimi/Shutterstock.com, p. 75; Andresr/Shutterstock.com, p. 63; Andy Lyons/Getty Images, p. 66; © AP Images, p. 68, 83, 92; BSIP/UIG via Getty Images, pp. 34, 53; catwalker/Shutterstock.com, p. 46; Cultura Science/Sigrid Gombert/Getty Images, p. 84; D Dipasupil/ FilmMagic/Getty Images, p. 10; DEA PICTURE LIBRARY/De Agostini Editorial/Getty Images, p. 51; Denise Truscello/WireImage/Getty Images, p. 27; Designua/Shutterstock.com, p. 37; extender_01/Shutterstock.com, pp. 3, 6; Golden Pixels LLC/Shutterstock.com, p. 78; /Joao Paulo Burini/Moment/Getty Images, p. 22; Joe Amon/Denver Post/Getty Images, p. 44; joshya/Shutterstock.com, p. 44; KaninRoman/iStock/Thinkstock, p. 70; LAGUNA DESIGN/Science Photo Library/Getty Images, p. 31; Mina De La O/Digital Vision/Getty Images, p. 29; Monkey Business Images/Shutterstock.com, p. 33; NaiyanaDonraman/iStock/Thinkstock, p. 49; Pat Greenhouse/The Boston Globe via Getty Images, p. 90; PathDoc/Shutterstock.com, p. 39; Paul Irish/Toronto Star/Getty Images, p. 14; petr73/Shutterstock.com, p. 61; Rafe Swan/Cultura/Getty Images, p.87; Ron Bull/Toronto Star/Getty Images, p. 24; rSnapshotPhotos/Shutterstock.com, p. 57; science photo/Shutterstock.com, p. 54; Sebastian Kaulitzki/Shutterstock.com, p. 40; The Washington Post/The Washington Post/Getty Images, p. 93; Tom Williams/CQ-Roll Call Group/Getty Images, p. 81; U.S. National Library of Medicine, History of Medicine Division, pp. 18, 20; withGod/Shutterstock.com, p. 59.

Cover Credits: extender_01/Shutterstock.com (sickle cells).

Contents

Sickle Cell Disease at a Glance 7

1 Trouble in the Blood 9

2 The History of Sickle Cell Disease 16

3 Living With Sickle Cell 26

4 Detecting and Treating the Disease 48

5 Prevention and a Cure 65

6 The Future of Sickle Cell Research 80

Top 10 Questions and Answers 94

Timeline of Sickle Cell Disease 97

Chapter Notes 100

Glossary 104

For More Information 108

Further Reading 109

Index 110

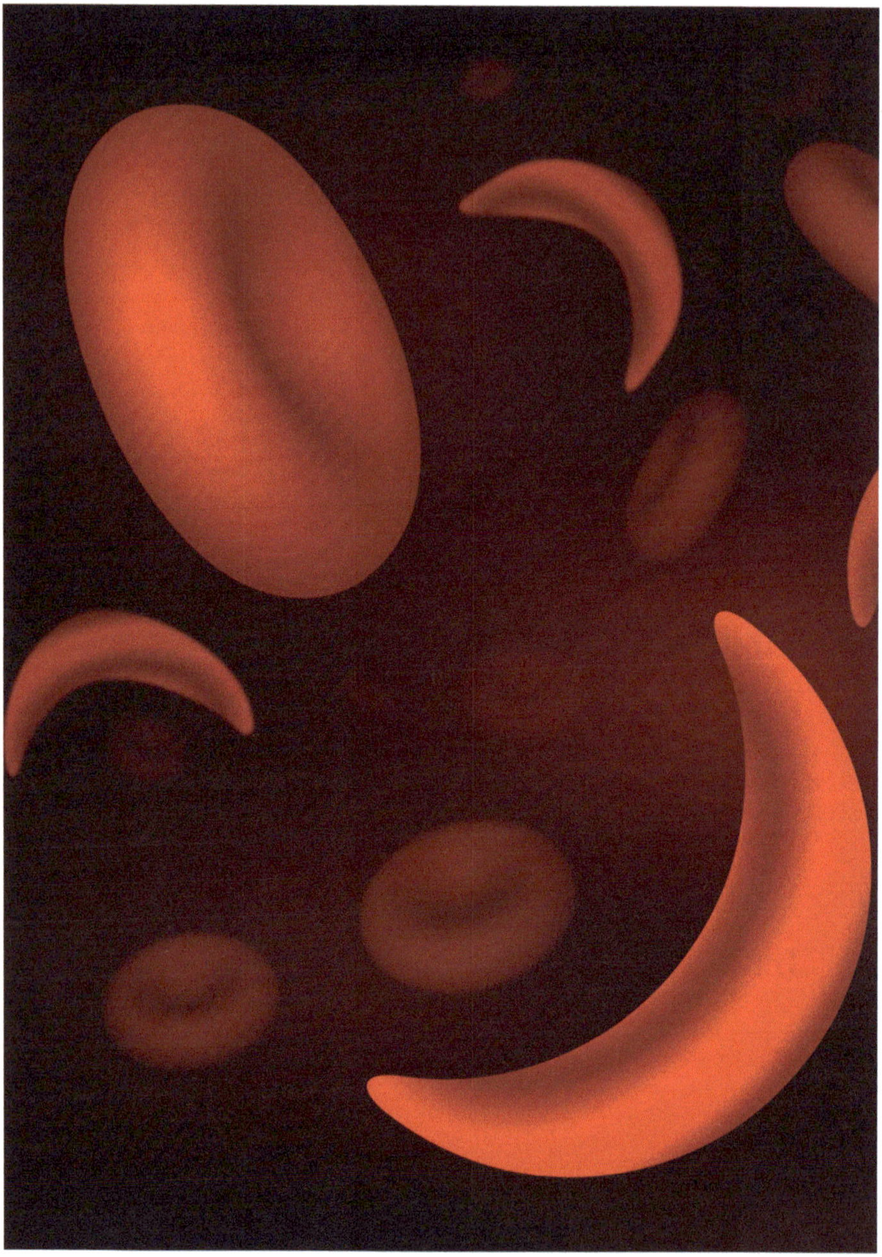

Normal red blood cells are round. The red blood cells of sickle cell disease are shaped like sickles, or crescents.

Sickle Cell Disease at a Glance

WHAT IS IT?

A disease that affects the red blood cells. Some of the red blood cells become sickle-shaped. These sickle cells become stiff and "sticky" and they clump together, blocking small blood vessels. Then body cells do not get enough oxygen.

WHO GETS IT?

Mainly Africans, African Americans, and Hispanics, but it is also found in people from the Mediterranean, the Caribbean, the Middle East, India, and Southeast Asia. It usually appears in childhood but may not cause symptoms until later.

HOW DO YOU GET IT?

By inheriting it from your parents. It is not contagious and is not spread by germs.

WHAT ARE THE SYMPTOMS?

The most common symptoms are tiredness, jaundice (yellowing of the skin and eyes), painfully swollen hands and feet, enlarged spleen, pains in the joints, frequent colds and other infections, slowed growth, and periods of intense pain.

HOW IS IT TREATED?

Daily penicillin and vaccination against pneumonia help protect children with sickle cell anemia from dangerous infections. Painkillers and drinking lots of fluids help to ease periods of intense pain. Drugs prevent the formation of sickle cells. Blood transfusions help prevent stroke.

IS THERE A CURE?

Bone marrow transplants have cured some people of sickle cell disease. However, it is difficult to find a perfect donor match, and the procedure is risky. Researchers are still pursuing a more widely available cure.

HOW CAN IT BE PREVENTED?

Programs for screening newborns can identify people at risk for sickle cell disease to help prevent serious symptoms; screening and counseling can help in family planning.

1 Chapter

Trouble in the Blood

Tionne "T-Boz" Watkins is the "T" in TLC, a popular music group in the 1990s that sold millions of records and earned four Grammy awards. Kier Spates is a successful actor and comedian, known to millions as Junior on the *Steve Harvey Morning Show*. But T-Boz and Kier have something else in common, besides high-profile careers in the entertainment business. They both suffer from a blood disorder known as sickle cell disease.

At just eight years old, T-Boz was diagnosed with the disorder. She was told that she would not be able to live out her dream of singing and dancing. But she refused to listen. As a teenager, T-Boz was determined not to let sickle cell disease control her life. Positive attitude is the key, she believes. It isn't always easy, though. There are times when she has really bad days. "Sickle cell is very excruciating pain," T-Boz says. "It feels like somebody is stabbing

T-Boz, seen here performing in 2014, is able to manage her sickle disease and live a full life.

OXYGEN IN THE BLOOD

Sickle cell disease is often called sickle cell anemia because anemia is a typical effect of the disease. Anemia is a serious loss of red blood cells. Not enough red blood cells means not enough oxygen is getting to the body's cells. A person who is anemic may feel faint, dizzy, or drowsy.

you over and over again. There are sharp pains in my legs, where I can't walk." Sometimes she has to go to the hospital. There she receives pain medication and breathes through an oxygen mask to help her recover.

In 1996 T-Boz decided to go public about her condition. She became the national spokesperson for the Sickle Cell Disease Association of America (SCDAA). As spokesperson, T-Boz educates people about the disease and helps raise money for sickle cell research. She also tells people about the importance of having a positive attitude, even when times are tough.

For T-Boz, her treatment involves eating lots of fruits and vegetables, exercising regularly, taking vitamins, including a daily dose of folic acid. (Folic acid helps to make more red blood cells.) Drinking plenty of fluids helps, too.

In 2000 T-Boz gave birth to her daughter, Chase. She calls Chase her "miracle baby" because she was told she couldn't have children. (Sickle cell disease can damage a person's organs, including the reproductive organs.) Chase, who is now a teenager, did not inherit the disease.

In 2013 T-Boz starred in the reality show *Totally T-Boz*, about reinventing herself as a solo artist.

T-Boz knows how difficult it is to live with sickle cell anemia. But she refuses to give up hope and she tells others to do the same. The best way for people to deal with the disease, she says, is to educate themselves.[1]

Sickle cell anemia is the most common genetic disease in the United States today. Still, most people know very little about it. Comedian and actor Kier Spates went public about his condition in 2013. Now he donates his time to the Rise Above campaign, to help raise public awareness about sickle cell disease. In 2013 Spates became the national celebrity ambassador to the Sickle Cell Disease Association of America. His job is to help get the word out about why people living with sickle cell anemia need attention and support.

WHAT IS A SICKLE CELL?

Sickle cell anemia is a blood disease. Sometimes the red blood cells change from their normal, round shape to a long, curved shape that looks like the blade of a sickle. (A sickle is a garden tool used to cut grass or grain.) That is how the disease got its name.

Sickle cell anemia is a blood disease. Sometimes the red blood cells change from their normal, round shape to a long, curved shape that looks like the blade of a sickle.

People with sickle cell anemia often have painful crises, or episodes of intense pain. These pain crises are caused by the formation of sickle cells, which pile up and

IRON OVERLOAD

People sometimes take iron supplements to combat anemia. Taking iron supplements will not help people with sickle cell disease. This type of anemia is not caused by too little iron in the blood; it is caused by not having enough red blood cells. In fact, taking iron supplements could harm a person with sickle cell disease because the extra iron builds up in the body and can cause damage to the organs.

block the flow of blood through the body. Sometimes the pain becomes so unbearable that people with sickle cell anemia have to go to the hospital.

Sickle cell anemia is a chronic disease. People with the disease have to live with it for the rest of their lives.

Sickle cell anemia affects millions of people all over the world. It is most common in people whose families come from parts of Africa. But it also occurs in South America, Central America, Cuba, Saudi Arabia, India, and Mediterranean countries (such as Spain, Portugal, Turkey, Greece, and Italy). Sickle cell anemia is the most common genetic disease in the United States, where it affects about 100,000 people. Most of them are African Americans, but the disease can also affect other races.[2]

Sickle cell anemia is a chronic disease. *Chronic* means ongoing. People with the disease have to live with it for the

Children born with sickle cell disease live longer, more productive lives because of the treatments available.

THE COST OF IGNORANCE

Sickle cell anemia is not widely understood. Advocates of sickle cell patients stress the importance of raising awareness about the disease. During a crisis, a patient may suffer a degree of pain unimaginable to most people. Repeated crises mean that patients often miss school and work days, yet individuals with sickle cell have lost their jobs because their employers think they are just slacking off. Even emergency room doctors have been slow to offer painkillers because they assume a patient is abusing drugs. Caucasians with sickle cell anemia have faced disbelief about their condition, because people assume the disorder only affects African Americans. Educating everyone about sickle cell disease can help improve the lives of people with this condition.

rest of their lives. Before the 1970s, the outlook for sickle cell patients was not very good. It was not uncommon for children born with the disease to die at an early age because of complications. Many patients were not expected to live past their twenties. These days, however, early detection and better treatments have made it possible for children with sickle cell anemia to grow up to live longer, more productive lives.

2 Chapter

The History of Sickle Cell Disease

Sickle cell disease was present in Africa long before it was first "discovered" in the western hemisphere. This ancient illness was known by different names in many tribal languages. However, symptoms of the disease were first described in the United States just over a century ago.

In September 1904, Walter Clement Noel, a twenty-year-old man from the West Indian island of Grenada, boarded a ship headed for the United States. He wanted to become a dentist and get his education at the Chicago College of Dental Surgery. During the voyage, Noel noticed a sore on his ankle, which became quite painful. When the ship docked in New York, Noel decided to go to a doctor, who gave him iodine to heal his wound. He then continued his journey to Chicago, where he became a dental student.

Near the end of November, Noel developed a serious chest infection. For a while, he suffered through his symptoms. The day after Christmas, though, he was feeling weak and dizzy, and went to the Presbyterian Hospital in Chicago. There Dr. Ernest E. Irons, a young hospital intern, took Noel's medical history and gave him a routine physical exam. He also took blood and urine samples. When Dr. Irons examined the blood sample, he noticed that some of the red blood cells looked strange, like nothing he had ever seen before. Dr. Irons then informed the attending physician on duty, heart specialist Dr. James Herrick, about his unusual findings.

Dr. Herrick listened to Noel's complaints of shortness of breath, heart palpitations, constant coughing, and aches and pains in his muscles. Noel also felt tired all the time, had headaches, bouts of dizziness, and he had sores on his legs. He told the doctor that he had had many of these symptoms since he was about ten years old. After writing down these symptoms, Dr. Herrick took another sample of Noel's blood and looked at it under a microscope. He thought that the patient had a kind of anemia, a serious loss of red blood cells. But this was not like any anemia he had seen before. To his surprise, many of the red blood cells had an odd shape. They were not tiny and round like red blood cells were supposed to be. They were long and curved, like crescents or sickles. Dr. Irons drew a rough sketch of these strange-looking red blood cells—the first pictures of sickle cells.

Dr. Herrick spent the next few years caring for his patient as best as he could, while studying this strange disease. Noel had to be treated in a hospital a number of times, but he still managed to finish his dental training. He went back home to Grenada in 1907 and set up a dental

Dr. James Herrick treated the first known person in America with sickle cell disease.

practice. However, Noel died from chest problems resulting from the disease at the age of thirty-two.

In 1910 Dr. Herrick reported his observations of Walter Clement Noel's unusual case in the scientific journal *Archives of Internal Medicine*. He became the first person to publish a medical report on the condition that was later named sickle cell disease.[1]

A MYSTERIOUS DISEASE

After Dr. Herrick published his report, other doctors observed patients with similar symptoms. A second case of unusual anemia with sickle-shaped cells was reported in 1911, a third case in 1915, and a fourth in 1922. All these new cases seemed to fit a definite pattern: Many patients had an African ancestry, and the disease appeared to be hereditary, since it affected parents as well as their children. As a number of other new cases continued to trickle in, doctors became desperate to uncover the mysteries of this strange illness.

The term sickle cell anemia was first used in 1922, by Verne Mason, a doctor at Johns Hopkins Hospital in Baltimore, Maryland.

The term *sickle cell anemia* was first used in 1922, by Verne Mason, a doctor at Johns Hopkins Hospital in Baltimore, Maryland. After studying the first four case reports of this unknown disease, Mason noted similarities among the patients. Among them, he pointed out that they were all of African origin. This observation may have started the popular misconception that the disease affected only those with African ancestry.

Verne Mason was one of the first people to identify similarities among people with sickle cell anemia.

In 1923 John Huck, an instructor at the Johns Hopkins University Medical School, became one of the first people to study heredity's role in sickle cell anemia. Huck studied information from two families. He concluded that sickle cell anemia is an inherited condition.

In 1933 Dr. Lemuel W. Diggs, professor at the University of Tennessee College of Medicine in Memphis, explained that not all people who can form sickle cells get the disease. Those with sickle cell anemia have periods when many red blood cells "sickle," and they often experience unbearable pain. There are also people who have inherited a tendency to form sickle cells from one parent but not from the other. They are said to have the sickle cell trait. These people rarely develop symptoms because they do not have enough sickled cells to have an effect on the body. People with the sickle cell trait can live long, productive lives without any harmful effects of the disease.

A CONVERSATION ON THE TRAIN

In 1945 two Nobel Prize winners, Dr. William B. Castle, an expert on anemias, and Dr. Linus Pauling, a well-known chemist, took a train ride together and happened to talk about sickle cell anemia. Castle told Pauling about how the cells in sickle cell patients sickled more when oxygen levels were low. Pauling thought that hemoglobin, a chemical in red blood cells that carries oxygen, might be the key to the sickling problem.

Intrigued by the conversation with Dr. Castle, Dr. Pauling, along with his colleagues, did further research on sickle cell anemia. They found that an abnormal form of hemoglobin was indeed causing red blood cells to sickle. When the cells change their shape, they become sticky and

HOW SICKLE CELL SURVIVED

Researchers have learned that people with the sickle cell trait, not the illness itself, seem to be protected against a deadly disease called malaria. Malaria is caused by a parasite that lives inside red blood cells. The parasite is carried by certain mosquitoes found in the tropics, especially Africa. These mosquitoes can pass the disease to people through their bite. Scientists have found that people with the sickle cell trait are more likely to survive malaria outbreaks than average people, or even those with sickle cell disease. As a result, the sickle cell trait has survived through the years, passing from one generation to the next.

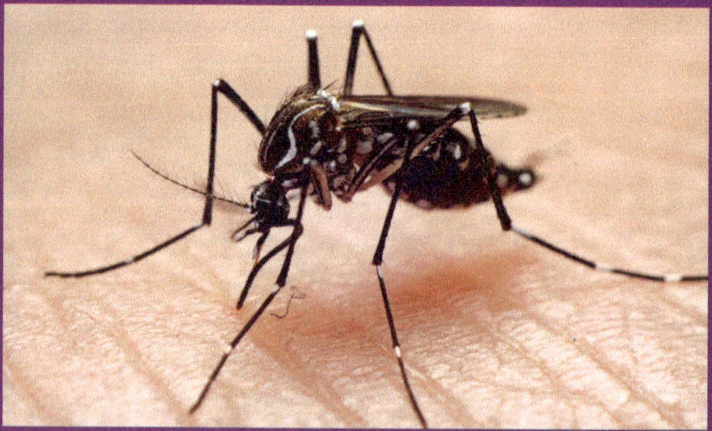

Malaria is passed to people by the bite of a mosquito carrying the disease. People with sickle cell trait have extra protection against malaria.

clump together. Some of these abnormal blood cells are destroyed in the spleen, an organ that filters the blood for harmful substances. When red blood cells are destroyed, their total number drops. This causes anemia. Other sickle cells clog up the blood vessels, causing damage and pain to surrounding tissues, which are no longer receiving enough oxygen.

Soon Dr. Pauling was able to determine which people had the sickle cell trait and which had sickle cell anemia. The blood of people with the sickle cell trait contains a mixture of normal and abnormal hemoglobin. Dr. Pauling used a technique called *electrophoresis* to separate the two types of hemoglobin. A small sample of blood was placed on a gel-coated microscope slide. It was then placed in an electric field, and the different chemicals in the mixture moved along the slide at different speeds, forming separate spots. Once the hemoglobins were separated, Dr. Pauling was able to test for sickle hemoglobin.

A CHEMICAL CHANGE

In 1956, another scientist, Dr. Vernon Ingram, used Dr. Pauling's tests to find the key difference between normal and abnormal hemoglobin. Like other proteins, hemoglobin is made up of chains of smaller chemical building blocks, called *amino acids*. These chains are folded and looped in a complicated structure. Dr. Ingram used chemicals to break some of the bonds in the hemoglobin molecule. This treatment turned the molecule into a mixture of shorter amino acid chains. By separating these pieces and sorting them out, it was possible to work out a map of the protein's structure.

Dr. Linus Pauling, a two-time Nobel Prize winner, developed a test to determine whether a patient had sickle cell disease or sickle cell trait.

After comparing a normal hemoglobin molecule to an abnormal one, Dr. Ingram discovered that the two proteins had different amino acids in one spot on the chain. That single tiny change in the hemoglobin molecule seemed to be the cause of the sickling. It seems amazing that such a small difference could cause so many harmful effects in the body. Sickle cell anemia was the first hereditary disease for which the chemical change that caused it was known.

3 Chapter

Living With Sickle Cell

Sickle cell anemia is a debilitating disease. Yet many people afflicted with this disorder manage to lead active and fulfilling lives. AJ Green has accomplished an incredible amount in his life. A gifted singer, by age nineteen he had performed for presidents Clinton and Obama, sung live onstage with Elton John, performed a duet with Jennifer Hudson, and released an album of his music. What makes this even more amazing is that AJ suffers from sickle cell anemia.

AJ experienced his first pain crisis when he was just eight months old. He was screened for sickle cell anemia as a newborn, and AJ's parents knew he had the disease. When his foot began to hurt they took him to the doctor right away. AJ spent his childhood in and out of Las Vegas hospitals being treated for his condition. He started singing in church at age five, and found that music helped him to find relief from the pain. As this positive role model for

AJ Green is joined by singer Celine Dion at an event to raise money for sickle cell research.

other young people with sickle cell reminds us, "We don't know our personal expiration date. We should all live each day—really live it."[1]

FROM PARENT TO CHILD

Sickle cell anemia is not caused by a germ. People cannot "catch" the disease from someone who has it, the way they would a cold. Sickle cell anemia is hereditary. That means that the disease can be passed from parents to their children through their genes. Genes are chemicals that carry information determining a person's traits, such as curly hair, brown eyes, or big feet. In sickle cell anemia, a change in a gene causes red blood cells to change their shape—

THE ALPHABET BLOCKS OF LIFE

Everything about you—the color of your hair, the shape of your nose, even your blood type—is determined by chemicals called genes. *Genes contain very long chains of a chemical called* DNA (deoxyribonucleic acid). *DNA is made up of four kinds of building blocks, which spell out all the body's hereditary information the way the letters of the alphabet spell out, or put in "code," words and sentences. Your genetic code spells out everything that makes you who you are.*

The genes direct the formation of proteins from simple chemical units called amino acids. *There are about twenty different kinds of amino acids in human cells. They form their own "alphabet," spelling out proteins. Each time a cell divides, all of its genes are copied to make another set for the new cell. Sometimes mistakes are made in copying, resulting in changes in the proteins spelled out by the genes.*

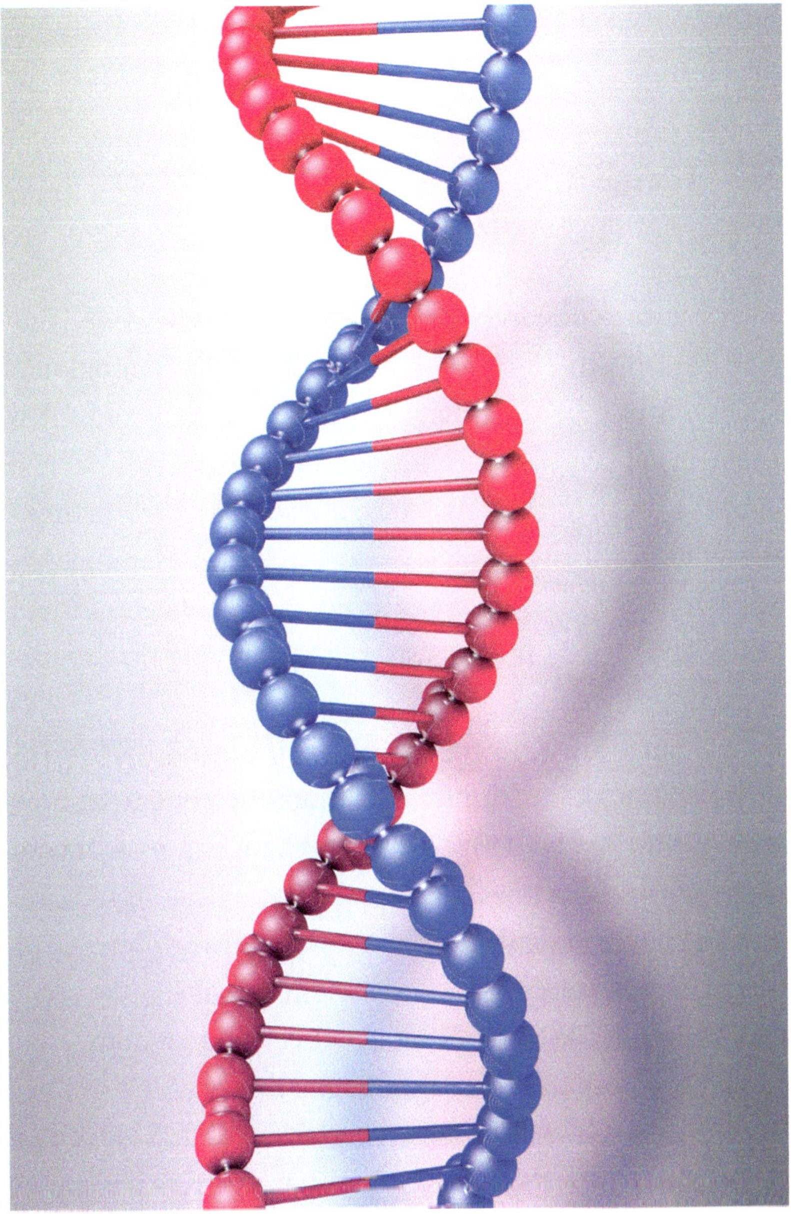

Sickle cell disease is hereditary. It is passed from parent to child through genes, which contain DNA. This illutration shows what a strand of DNA looks like.

from soft, round cells that look like doughnuts to long, curved, stiff cells that look like sickles or crescents.

Sickle cell anemia is not caused by a germ. People cannot "catch" the disease from someone who has it.

A person with sickle cell anemia has a faulty gene. This gene controls the formation of hemoglobin. Hemoglobin is an iron-rich protein that gives blood its red color. It is found in all red blood cells. Hemoglobin carries oxygen from the lungs to the body cells. It also takes carbon dioxide waste from the body cells to the lungs. Hemoglobin picks up these gases very easily, but it also lets go of them easily. That is why it works so well in carrying these gases through the body.

A change in just one "letter" in the gene that forms part of hemoglobin results in a dramatic change in how hemoglobin works. This one-letter change is what causes sickle cell anemia.

Normal hemoglobin is known as hemoglobin A, or Hb A. People with sickle cell anemia make a different kind, hemoglobin S (Hb S). A number of other changes in hemoglobin can also cause problems that lead to sickling, but Hb S is the most common. Hemoglobin S does not carry as much oxygen as Hb A. When there is not much oxygen in the blood, the hemoglobin S molecules stick together, forming stiff fibers. These fibers change the shape of the red blood cells into long, curved sickles.

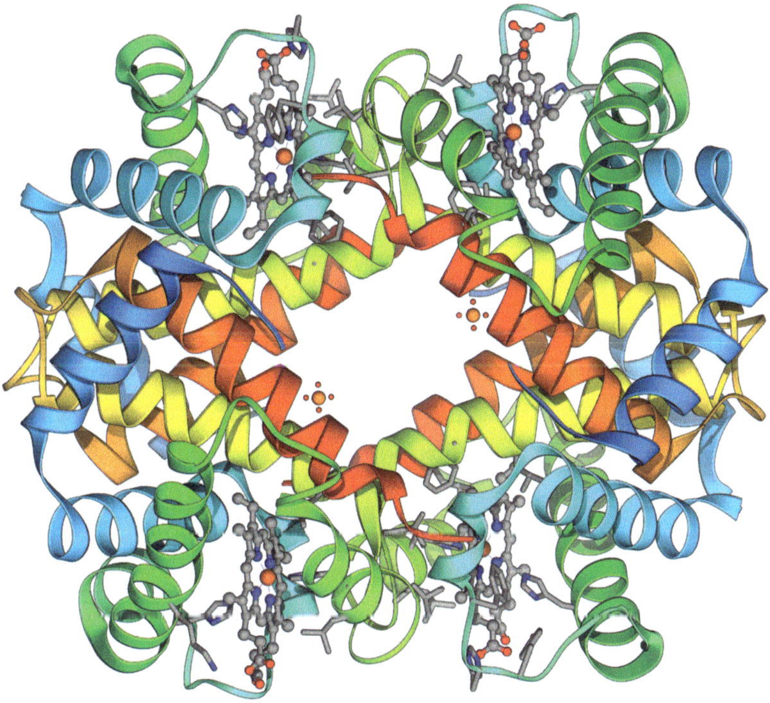

Hemoglobin, illustrated here, is a protein in the blood. The hemoglobin found in the blood of people with sickle cell anemia does not contain as much oxygen as normal hemoglobin.

SICKLE CELL TRAIT

Sickle cell anemia will develop in a child only if he or she inherits one sickle cell gene from the mother and one sickle cell gene from the father. People who inherit one normal hemoglobin gene and one faulty hemoglobin gene will carry the sickle cell trait. More than 2 million Americans carry the sickle cell trait.[2]

People sometimes confuse sickle cell anemia with sickle cell trait. People with the sickle cell trait are carriers. Usually they do not have any symptoms or problems from the disease. Carriers do have sickle hemoglobin (Hb S), just like those with the disease. However, the amount is fairly low, about 30 percent Hb S. (A person with sickle cell anemia may have 80 percent or more Hb S.) The rest of a carrier's hemoglobin is normal (Hb A). This is enough to do a good job of carrying oxygen and carbon dioxide.

Usually people with sickle cell trait are free of symptoms of the disease. However, symptoms may develop under certain unusual conditions. For example, extreme stress, lack of oxygen, a high altitude (such as climbing a mountain), extreme heat or cold, or dehydration (loss of fluids) after exercise might cause red blood cells to sickle. This does not mean that the person has developed the disease. Still, athletes with sickle cell trait should take care not to overwork themselves.

Carriers should be aware, too, that their sickle cell trait can be passed on to their children.

THE COMPONENTS OF BLOOD

Because sickle cell anemia is a blood disease, it would help to understand it better if you know what goes on in your blood.

INHERITING SICKLE CELL

Genes are lined up like beads on a necklace in structures called chromosomes. A complete set of chromosomes (forty-six in humans) is found in each body cell. Chromosomes come in pairs, and thus there are usually at least two genes for each trait, one inherited from each parent. Some genes are dominant—their effects are seen even if only one of the particular genes is present. Some genes are recessive—their effects appear only if two recessive genes are inherited, one from each parent. Sickle cell anemia is caused by a recessive gene for an abnormal form of hemoglobin. Therefore, this disease develops only when a person receives a sickle cell gene from ***both*** *parents.*

Sickle cell disease can be passed down through generations of a family.

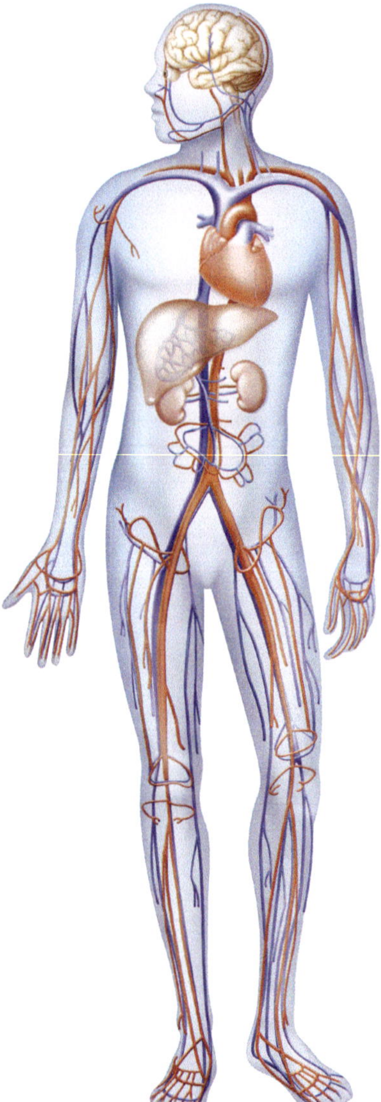

The circulatory system consists of the heart, arteries, veins, and blood.

Blood is made up of four main parts: 1) plasma, 2) red blood cells, 3) white blood cells, and 4) platelets. Plasma is the liquid part of the blood—it makes up more than half of the blood. Red blood cells float in the plasma. They carry oxygen from the lungs to the body cells. White blood cells, which fight infection, and platelets, which are parts of cells that help stop bleeding, are also found in the plasma.

Blood can reach every part of your body through a system of tubes called blood vessels. The blood circulates around the body over and over again, which is why the heart and blood vessels are called the circulatory system. As blood leaves the heart, it flows through large blood vessels, called arteries. (So remember this: *Arteries* and *Away* from the heart both start with the letter *A*.) The arteries branch into smaller and smaller blood vessels. The tiniest blood vessels are called capillaries. They are so small that you could not see them without a microscope, and they have very thin walls.

Oxygen and food materials pass out through the capillary walls and into the body cells. Waste products from the cells pass into the bloodstream and are carried away. Blood returns to the heart through veins, and the process starts all over again, with every heartbeat. It takes less than a minute for the blood to circulate all around the body. This happens more than a thousand times a day.

Meanwhile, blood also flows through a smaller circle of blood vessels that lead from the heart to the lungs and back again. The air you inhale (breathe in) contains oxygen, which body cells need to get energy from foods. It passes down into the lungs through branching tubes that look like an upside-down tree. The tiniest branches end in bubble-like air sacs. Like the capillaries, these air sacs have very thin walls. Each sac is surrounded by a net of capillaries. As blood flows by them, oxygen passes out through the walls of the air sacs and into the capillaries. The cells' waste products go from the capillaries into the air sacs, where they will be blown out the next time you exhale. One of the main waste products is a gas called carbon dioxide, which is formed when cells use food materials to produce energy.

Oxygen is carried in the blood mainly by the red blood cells. There are about 25 trillion red blood cells in an adult's body—more than 250 million in each drop of blood. Like most other body cells, they are microscopic, but they are actually wider than the openings inside the smallest capillaries. Red blood cells are soft and flexible. They can bend and twist to pass through the tiny capillaries. Eventually, though, they wear out. Red blood cells live for only about 120 days. The old, worn-out cells are broken down in the liver and spleen, and their chemicals are recycled.

Red blood cells are produced in the bone marrow, the spongy material that fills the spaces of the large bones. When the oxygen supply to the bone marrow is low, the bone marrow starts making more red blood cells. Each second, from two million to ten million red blood cells in a person's body are destroyed. An equal number of new red blood cells are produced in the bone marrow to replace them.

WHEN BLOOD CELLS CHANGE SHAPE

The abnormal hemoglobin (Hb S) produced in people with sickle cell anemia cannot carry as much oxygen as

WHY CELLS SICKLE

(1) *The person has Hb S instead of Hb A.*

(2) *Hb S does not hold as much oxygen as Hb A.*

(3) *With less oxygen, the red blood cells change into a sickle shape.*

(4) *The sickle-shaped cells clump together.*

(5) *Clumped cells block blood flow to tissues and organs, causing pain.*

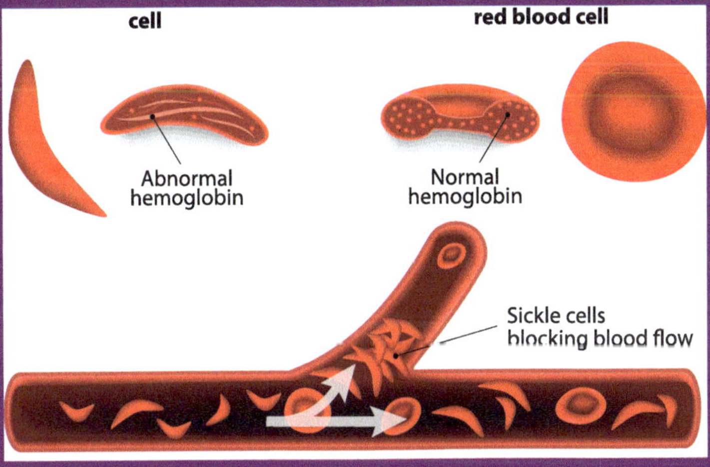

Sickle cells clump and block blood vessels.

normal hemoglobin. The lack of oxygen causes the red blood cells to change their shape from round and plump to long and curved, like the blade of a sickle. These sickle cells cannot bend and twist the way normal red blood cells can, and they cannot squeeze through the tiny capillaries. Instead, they become stiff and sticky. They get stuck in the narrow capillaries, and even in larger blood vessels. The sickle cells start to pile up in the blood vessels, clogging the openings. Fewer oxygen-carrying blood cells are able to get through, which leads to even more sickling.

People with sickle cell disease often develop anemia, a condition in which the number of red blood cells is below the normal level. Sickle cells are very brittle and tend to break apart easily. They have a very short life span—only ten to twenty days—compared to the 120-day life span of normal red blood cells. So it is very difficult for the bone marrow to make enough red blood cell replacements. As a result, not enough oxygen can get to the body's tissues—which leads to even more sickling. People who are anemic often feel tired and weak.

COMMON SYMPTOMS

Sickle-cell symptoms develop when the sickled cells plug up blood vessels. This prevents the oxygen-carrying blood from reaching important organs. Tissues near the blockage are starved of oxygen and nutrients.

The most common complaint in sickle cell anemia is the unbearable pain. People with sickle cell anemia have what they call pain crises, or episodes of intense pain. The pain can develop in any organ or joint in the body, but the most common areas include the arms, legs, abdomen, chest, and back. The symptoms vary greatly from person

WHAT PAIN SIGNALS

When cells are damaged, or are not getting the oxygen and food materials they need, they call for help. They send out chemical alarm signals to tell the body they are in trouble. These signals are sent to the brain, which translates them into feelings of pain. The more cells that are damaged, the stronger the signals—and the more it hurts. You probably think of pain as a bad thing. It can be good for the body, though, if you heed the warning and do something quickly to fix the problem.

People with sickle cell disease suffer from periods of great pain.

WHAT DOES YOUR SPLEEN DO?

The spleen plays a very important role in protecting people from infections. It is packed with disease-fighting cells that protect the body from germs. Sickled cells may become trapped in the spleen, blocking tiny blood vessels and resulting in damage to the tissues they nourish. This damage makes it less able to fight infection. The blockage of spleen blood vessels may also cause the spleen to enlarge (become larger than normal), filling the whole abdominal area, as blood is trapped inside it. A hard, enlarged spleen is a common symptom in children with sickle cell anemia.

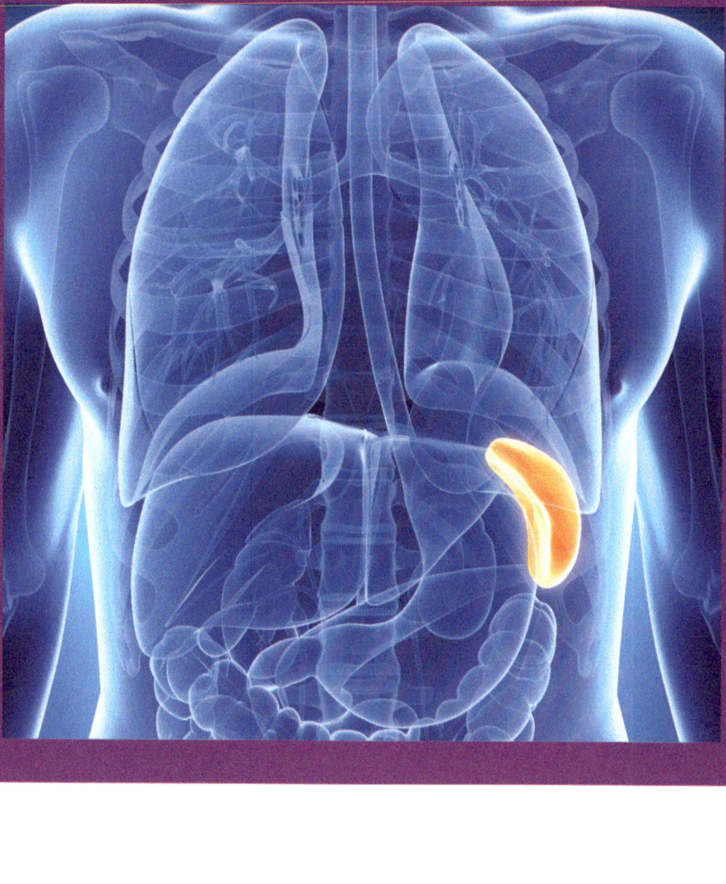

to person and even within the same person. One person may have only one crisis a year, while another may have one every few weeks. Some people may go for months or years without a crisis and then suddenly have one after another. A pain crisis usually lasts for a few hours to a few days, but sometimes it can last for weeks.

The most common complaint in sickle cell anemia is the unbearable pain. People with sickle cell anemia have what they call pain crises, or episodes of intense pain.

Sickle cell crises can have dangerous effects on the body. The lack of oxygen can damage important organs, such as the lungs, kidneys, and spleen. Sickle cells that cause narrowing and blockage in the blood vessels in the brain can cause a stroke. Brain cells that normally get oxygen and food materials from these blood vessels are starved. After just a few minutes without oxygen, they may begin to die. If many brain cells die, the person can no longer do the things those cells controlled—such as speaking or moving an arm or a leg.

This kind of stroke occurs mainly in children. About 30 percent of children with sickle cell disease have a stroke.[3] A stroke can lead to learning problems, and possibly even paralysis (loss of feeling or movement in a body part). Children with sickle cell disease also get sick more often than those without the disorder. They have a higher risk of developing serious illnesses, including pneumonia, meningitis, influenza, and hepatitis. Fever is an important early warning sign of illness. A fever of 101°F is a signal to call the doctor. If the fever rises to 103°F, the child should be rushed to the emergency room. Such a high fever may be caused by an infection in the blood. This can be very dangerous if it is not treated right away.

People with sickle cell disease may develop jaundice, a yellowing of the skin and eyes. This condition is not harmful itself, but it is a sign of a problem in the blood. When jaundice develops along with other symptoms, including nausea, vomiting, and abdominal pain, it could be a sign of gall bladder problems.

Acute chest syndrome may develop as a result of infection or trapped sickled cells in blood vessels in the lungs. Symptoms include chest pain, coughing, difficulty breathing, and fever.

Children with sickle cell anemia may grow more slowly than normal, so they are typically small for their age.

Some people develop sores that do not heal. These sores are usually seen in adults. They are brought on by poor blood circulation and typically occur on the ankles. Poor circulation is also the cause of painful joints that affect older people with sickle cell anemia. The cutoff of the blood supply to the eyes can be so severe that it may even cause blindness.

A very common symptom in young children is the hand-foot syndrome. As tiny blood vessels become blocked by sickled cells, the hands and feet swell and become hot, red, and painful.

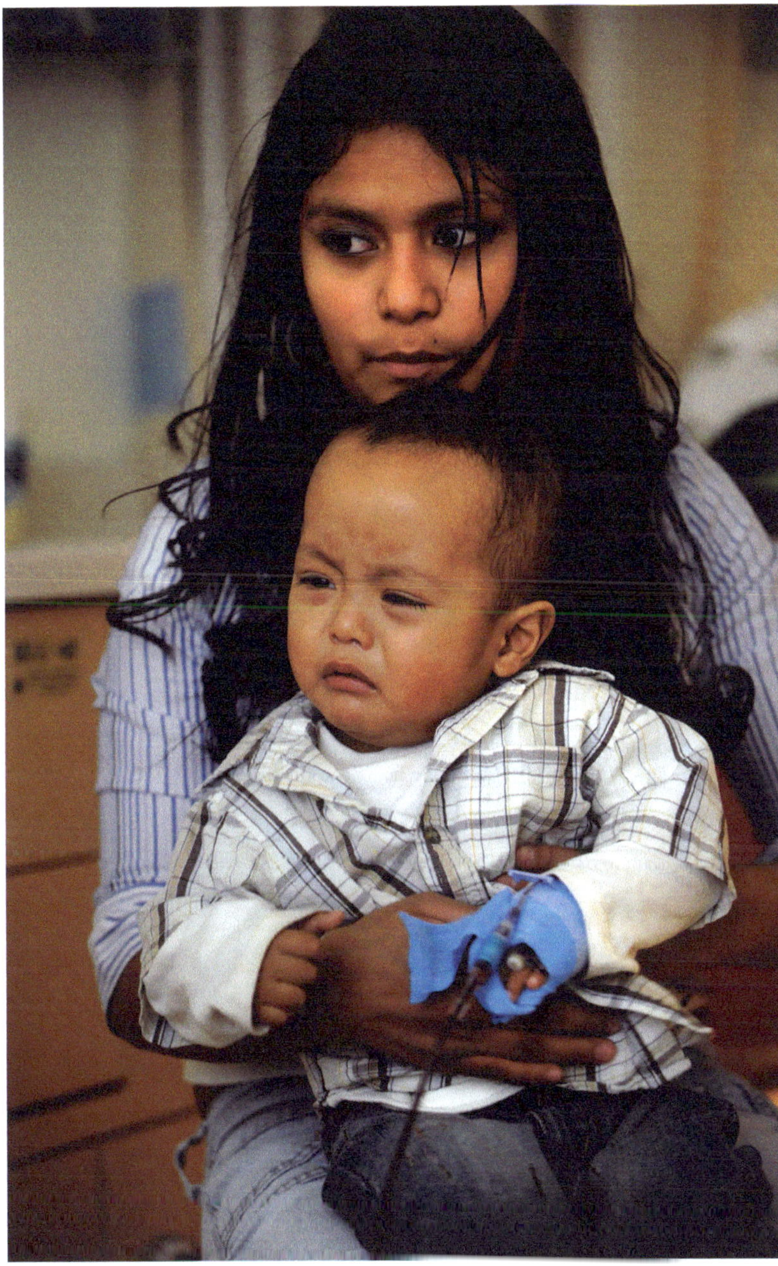

Children with sickle cell disease get sick more often than those without the disorder. One form of treatment for the disease is a monthly blood transfusion.

COMMON SIGNS AND SYMPTOMS OF THALASSEMIA

- *Pain in joints, bones, chest, abdomen, arms, legs (may be sudden, chronic, and/or intense)*
- *Feeling very tired and weak (due to anemia)*
- *Shortness of breath*
- *Jaundice (yellowing of the skin and eyes)*
- *Fever*
- *Headache*
- *Blurry vision*
- *Slow-healing sores on lower legs*
- *Swelling of abdomen (due to enlarged spleen)*
- *Bed-wetting*
- *In males: priapism, a painful erection that lasts for hours*

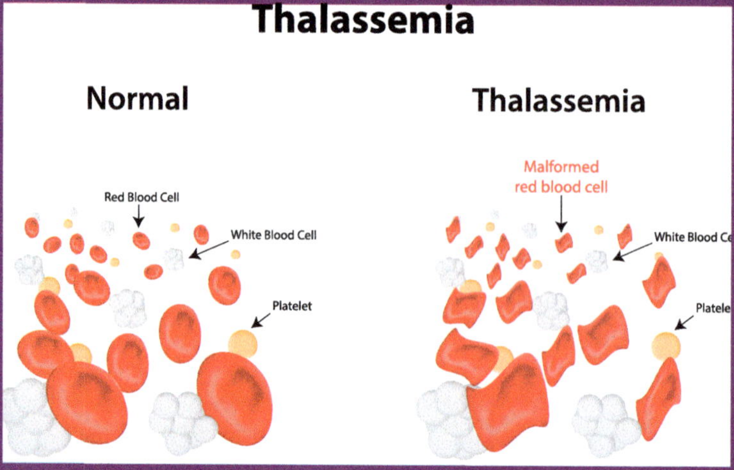

This diagram shows the difference in the shape of blood cells with thalassemia.

Children with sickle cell disease may also grow more slowly than normal, so they are typically small for their age, with an underdeveloped body.

ANOTHER INHERITED DISEASE: THALASSEMIA

Thalassemia, like sickle cell anemia, is an inherited disease that affects the hemoglobin in red blood cells. In thalassemia, there is not enough working hemoglobin to keep the body's organs supplied with oxygen. Anemia develops. Meanwhile, protein builds up inside the red blood cells. As a result, the cells become damaged and soon die, reducing the red blood cell supply.

In thalassemia, there is not enough working hemoglobin to keep the body's organs supplied with oxygen.

Thalassemia usually affects people from areas surrounding the Mediterranean Sea, such as Italy, Greece, and the Middle East. In fact, its name comes from the word *thalassa*, the Greek word for "sea." The disease also occurs in Americans of Italian, Greek, Middle Eastern, Southern Asian, and African ancestry.

The most severe form of thalassemia is thalassemia major, also known as Cooley's anemia, named after Dr. Thomas Cooley. It occurs when the genetic defect is inherited from both parents. Babies with this type of the disease may die if they are not properly treated. A milder form, thalassemia intermedia, occurs when a severe form is inherited from one parent or the mild form is inherited from both. It is not usually fatal. The mildest form is thalassemia minor. It occurs when the defect is inherited from

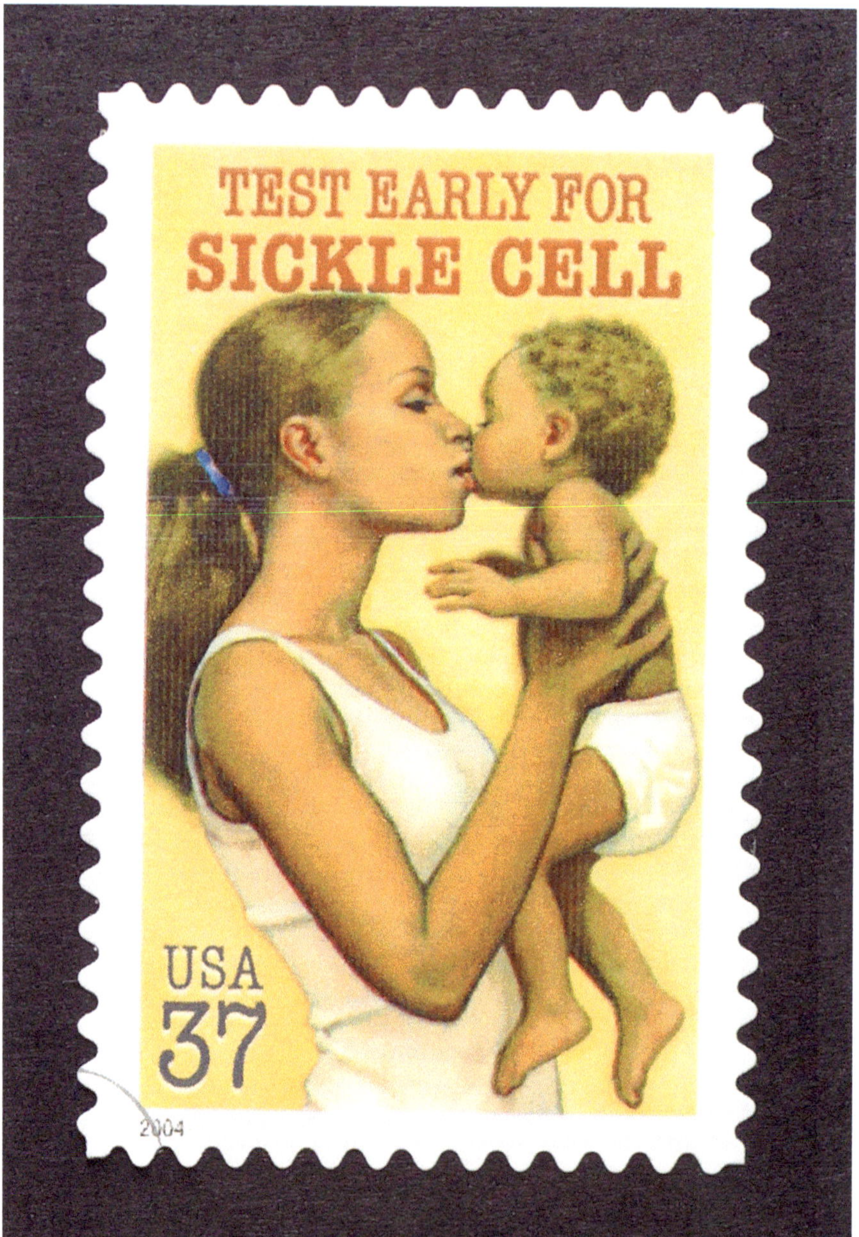

This U.S. postage stamp was released in 2004 to raise awareness for sickle cell disease.

only one parent. People with this form are carriers of the disease because they do not have any symptoms but may pass it on to their children. Thalassemia genes may also be combined with sickle cell genes, causing diseases with varying severity.

Symptoms of thalassemia are very much like sickle cell anemia. They may include tiredness, irritability, pale skin, poor appetite, and underdeveloped growth. A child may develop an enlarged heart, liver, and spleen.

Chapter 4

Detecting and Treating the Disease

If two parents are both carriers of the sickle cell trait, they have a one-in-four chance that their child will be born with sickle cell disease. Today all newborns are screened for the disease, but some don't begin to show symptoms until they are a year old. When Olive Downer was pregnant, she knew there was a 25 percent chance that her child could be born with sickle cell anemia. She and her husband were both carriers of the trait. After their daughter, Arianne, was born, the baby was tested for sickle cell anemia. The test came back negative, but the doctor told Olive that if her daughter had the disease, it would probably develop by the time she was a year old.

Arianne learned to walk when she was only nine months old. She showed no symptoms of the disease and seemed to be healthy. When Arianne was one year old, her parents breathed a sigh of relief—she still seemed to be free of the disease. When Arianne was two years old, however, she suddenly had trouble walking. She kept saying,

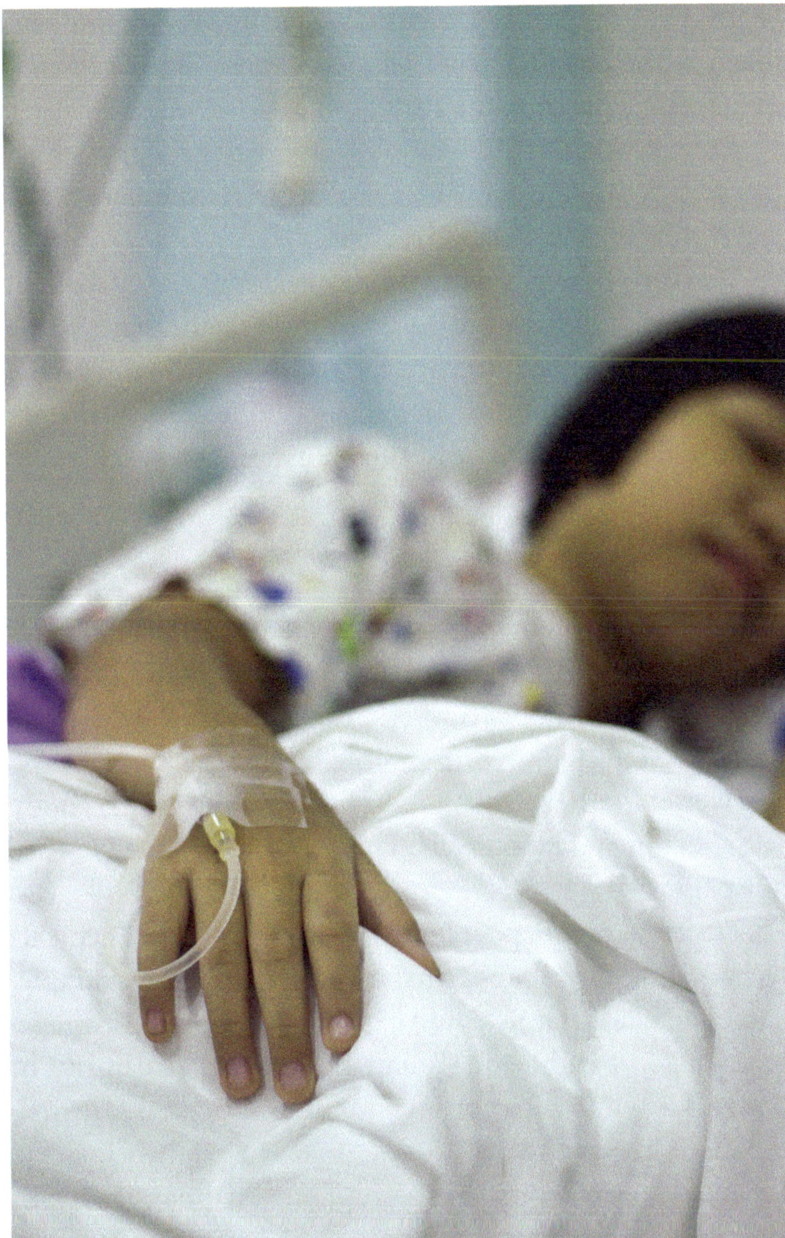

Patients with sickle cell disease who are suffering a pain crisis are often given medicine through a needle placed into a vein.

"Pain, pain . . ." as she pointed to her hips. Arianne was taken to the hospital, where they tested for sickle cell anemia again. This time the results were positive.

Olive worked with Arianne at home to get her back on her feet. With the help of a walker, Arianne eventually learned how to walk again.

During Arianne's early school years, she got frequent colds and a number of episodes of severe pain. Most of the time, Olive was able to care for Arianne at home, giving her over-the-counter medicine to ease the pain. However, about once or twice a year, the pain crises were so severe that she had to go to the hospital. There Arianne was hooked up to tubes dripping pain medicine into a vein in her arm until the pain went away.

From the ages of eleven to thirteen, her hospital stays averaged about fifteen times a year. On each visit, she had to stay from one to two weeks, depending on what body part was affected. During some of the visits, Arianne received blood transfusions, which supplied her body with healthy red blood cells. This treatment helped to ease her pain.[1]

Forty years ago, people with sickle cell disease typically had short life spans. In the early 1970s, for example, someone like Arianne could expect to live, on the average, to the age of eighteen.[2] Today, however, the majority of patients live into their forties and fifties.[3] Richard Mitchell, a patient at New York's Mount Sinai Hospital with sickle cell disease, celebrated his seventieth birthday in 2014.[4] Women with sickle cell anemia tend to live longer than men afflicted with the disorder. Doctors know much more about the disease than they did years ago. Accurate tests can give an early diagnosis, which is very important.

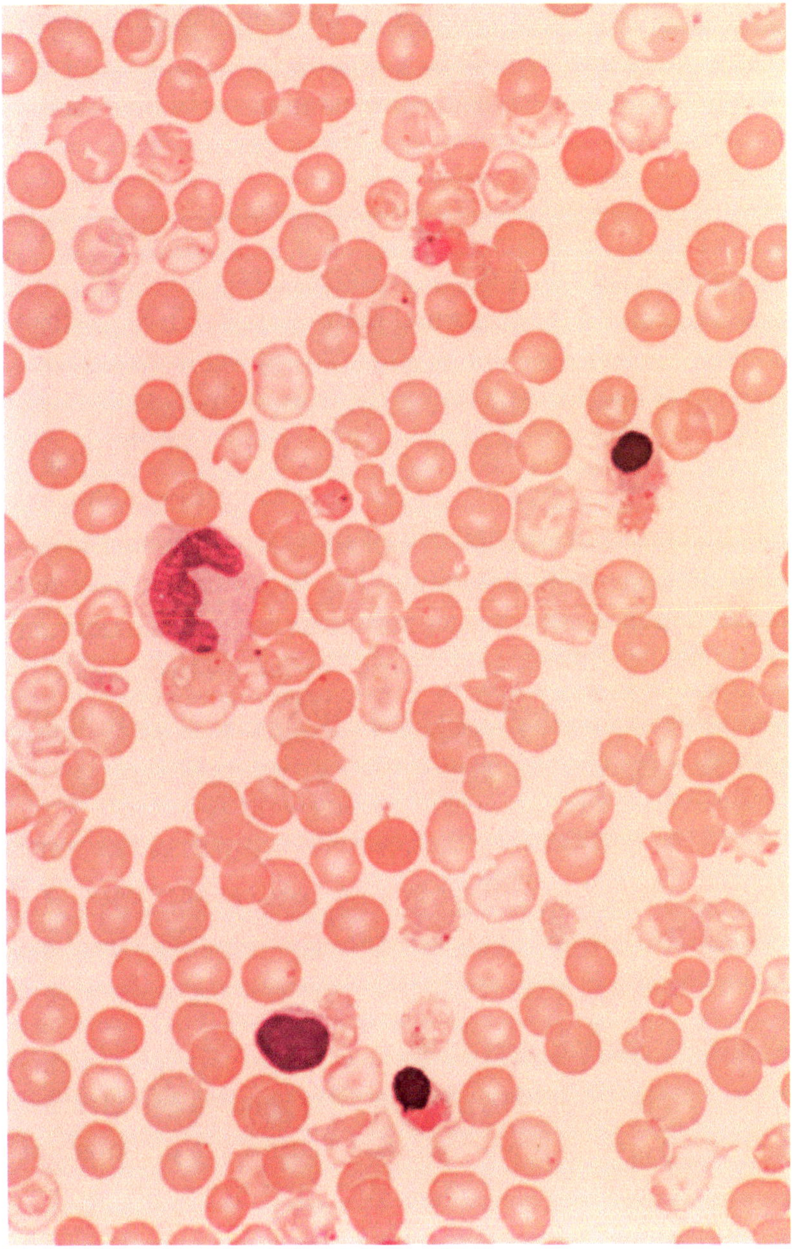

This is a view of sickle cells (in dark purple) as seen under a microscope.

Young children have a high risk for complications. Early treatment cannot only ease the pain, but it can also help prevent dangerous health problems that might develop.

A SIMPLE BLOOD TEST

A number of blood tests can be done to diagnose sickle cell anemia. One blood test is rather simple. It is used to screen the blood for abnormal hemoglobin (Hb S). A drop of blood is placed on a glass slide. The blood is mixed with a special chemical, which reduces the amount of oxygen it can hold. If there is Hb S in the blood, the lack of oxygen will change the shape of red blood cells into long, curved sickles. The sickle-shaped cells can be seen under a microscope. However, this test cannot tell the difference between people who have the disease and those who are carriers. In addition, this test does not work for babies because their blood does not contain enough Hb S to be picked up by the test.

Today, doctors know much more about sickle cell anemia than they did years ago. Accurate tests can give an early diagnosis, which is very important.

OTHER TYPES OF TESTS

There is a more effective blood test: hemoglobin electrophoresis. This test is widely used to confirm a diagnosis of sickle cell anemia. It is based on the test developed by Dr. Linus Pauling in the 1940s. This test is done by using an electric current to separate the different types of hemoglobin. Electrophoresis makes it possible to determine whether the patient has sickle cell trait or sickle cell

BENEFITS OF FETAL HEMOGLOBIN

At birth, and even before birth, the blood contains mainly fetal hemoglobin. Fetal hemoglobin seems to somehow protect the baby from sickle cell anemia. By six months of age, however, this hemoglobin is replaced witth adult hemoglobin. Sickle cell symptoms do not usually develop until after fetal hemoglobin is no longer in the blood. One drug currently helping many patients living with sickle cell disease is hydroxyurea. This drug increases the amount of fetal hemoglobin in the blood.

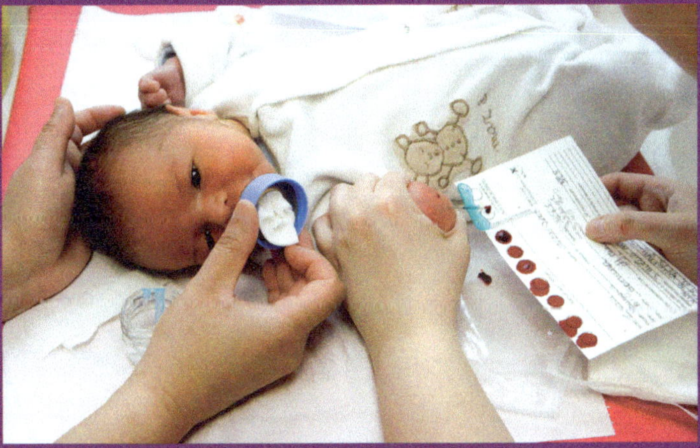

The fetal hemoglobin that babies are born with protects them from sickle cell disease. However, when the body replaces that with adult hemoglobin, babies at risk for the disease may begin showing symptoms of it.

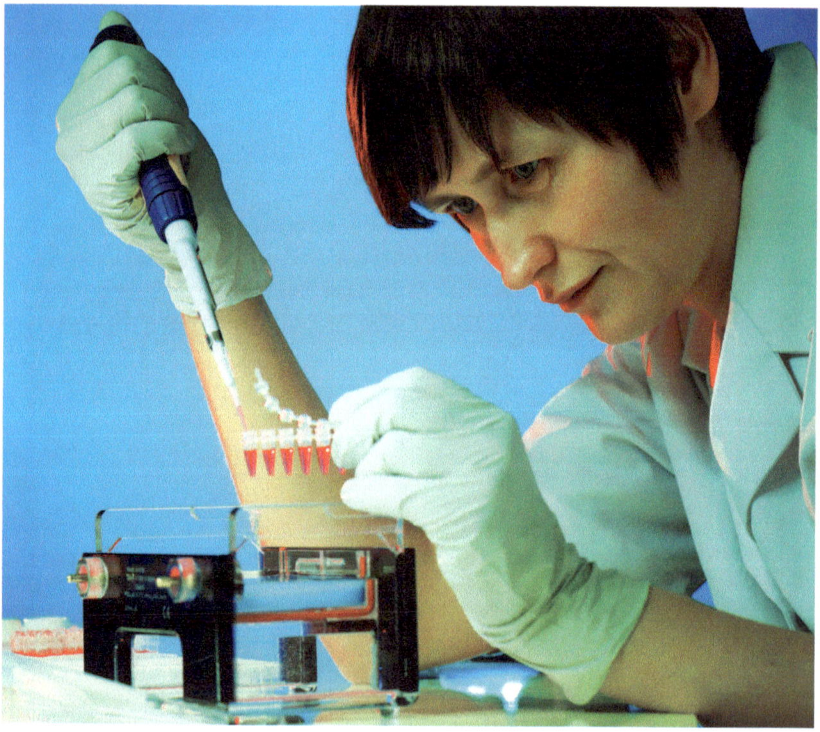

Electrophoresis is a process that allows doctors to determine if a person has sickle cell disease or sickle cell trait.

anemia. If the person has sickle cell trait, about 20 to 40 percent of the hemoglobin will be Hb S. A person with the disease will have from 80 to 100 percent Hb S.[5] This test can also detect other hemoglobin blood disorders, such as thalassemia. The hemoglobin electrophoresis test can also be used to diagnose babies.

An unborn baby can be tested for sickle cell disease using amniocentesis, which samples the amniotic fluid in the mother's womb. Another procedure used is chorionic villus sampling (CVS). Cells are extracted from the placenta, which contains the same genetic material as the fetus.

Blood tests can also provide additional information on the condition. For example, a complete blood count (CBC) gives the numbers of red blood cells as well as white blood cells. A low red blood cell (RBC) count is a sign of anemia. A high white blood cell (WBC) count shows that there is an infection in the body.

MANAGING PAIN

The main concern for sickle cell patients is controlling the pain. Some people find that over-the-counter painkillers can help ease the pain. Applying a warm cloth or a heating pad to the affected area may also help. Doctors also recommend lots of fluids and plenty of rest. However, these methods do not always work. If the pain cannot be controlled at home, a trip to the hospital may be necessary. There, patients may need to be given stronger pain medication, usually intravenously (a hollow needle is placed into a vein in the skin, and the medication flows through the needle and into the vein).

HEALTHY AVERAGES

Men normally have more red blood cells (RBCs) in their blood than women, and so they also have more hemoglobin (Hb). The averages for healthy adults are as follows:

Men: *RBCs 5.4 million per microliter of blood; Hb 14–18 grams per deciliter*
Women: *RBCs 4.8 million per microliter of blood; Hb 12–16 grams per deciliter*

(A microliter, or cubic millimeter, is about one-fiftieth of a drop of blood.)

In anemia, the number of red blood cells is about 17 percent less than the normal value, and there is also less hemoglobin. The averages for anemic adults are as follows:

Men: *RBCs less than 4.5 million per microliter; Hb less than 14 grams per deciliter*
Women: *RBCs less than 4 million per microliter; Hb less than 12 grams per deciliter*

Other treatment options are available. One current approach is hydroxyurea, a drug used to treat sickle cell disease. This drug may be given orally to patients who have frequent pain crises and show early signs of damage to organs. Hydroxyurea works by increasing the amount of fetal hemoglobin in the blood. Remember, this is the special form of hemoglobin that seems to protect against sickling. It is produced in a fetus and for about six months after birth. By one year of age, the amount of fetal hemoglobin in the blood has dropped from 80 percent to only 1 to 2 percent. Hydroxyurea can act on the cells that

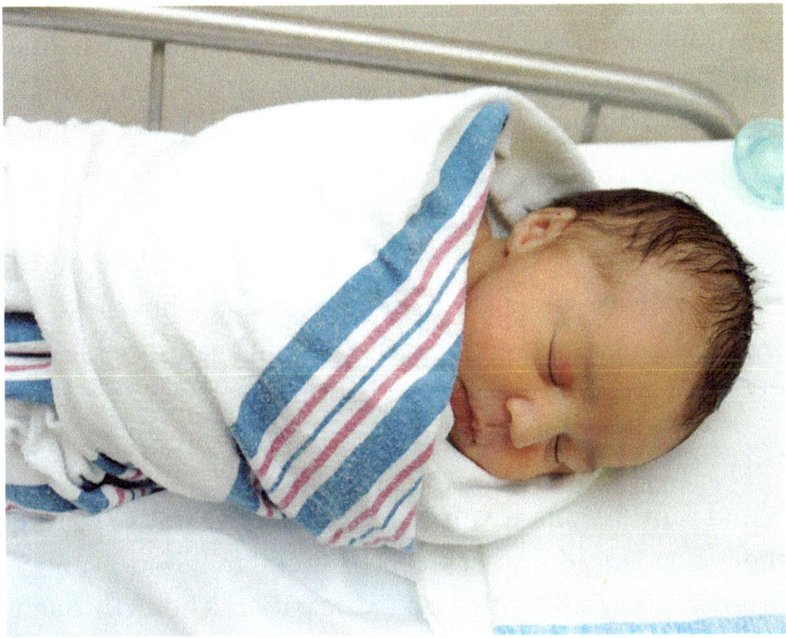

When babies are born, they have fetal hemoglobin, which protects their red blood cells from sickling. The drug hydroxyurea increases the amount of fetal hemoglobin in a person with sickle cell disease.

produce hemoglobin and actually increase the production of fetal hemoglobin. Studies have shown that hydroxyurea can significantly reduce the severity, as well as the number of pain crises.[6] This drug cannot stop a pain crisis once it has started, however—it can only prevent one from coming on. Hydroxyurea has also proven effective in reducing the number of transfusions needed by sickle cell patients.

Some patients do not tolerate hydroxyurea, which may cause side effects such as nausea, vomiting, hair loss, and lowered blood counts. Since the drug may cause birth defects, a patient should stop taking it if she becomes pregnant or plans to conceive a child. The long-term effects of hydroxyurea are still being studied, but the drug is now a front-line treatment in the fight against sickle cell disease.

BETTER BLOOD

Blood transfusions are often a very effective way to relieve the pain caused by sickle cell anemia. Blood from a healthy donor slowly flows into the patient's body through a hollow needle inserted into a vein. The job of blood transfusions is to increase the number of healthy red blood cells. This keeps the percentage of sickle cells below the level that may cause a pain crisis.

In a simple blood transfusion, donor blood is combined with the blood in the patient's body. In an exchange transfusion, the patient's blood is slowly replaced with a donor's healthy blood.

However, transfusions are not recommended as a routine way of relieving a person's pain crises. Not only are they inconvenient, there are some dangers involved. Regular blood transfusions can lead to a buildup of iron

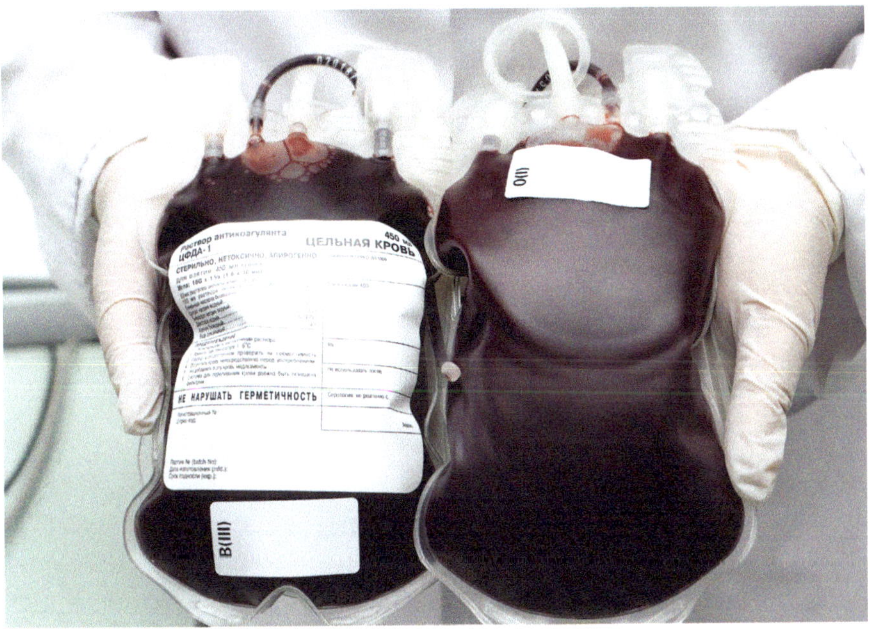

New, healthy blood is placed into a patient's body during a blood transfusion.

DIFFERENT BLOOD TYPES

Do you know what your blood type is? This refers to the kind of proteins on the surface of your red blood cells. Everybody has a combination of many different surface proteins (antigens), which are inherited from their parents. One "blood group" is called ABO: Some people have an A protein (type A blood), others a B (type B), some have neither (type O), and some have both (type AB).

What happens if a person with type O blood receives a transfusion of type A blood or type B blood? The person's body would begin to produce antibodies against the "foreign" antigen. Antibodies are proteins that normally attack invading germs and protect the body from harm. They fit together with antigens like a lock and key. Antibodies against the A antigen, for example, would grab hold of the antigens on red blood cells from a type A transfusion. The red blood cells would be destroyed. This kind of reaction occurs whenever the blood for a transfusion is not correctly matched to the patient's blood, but it is even more likely in sickle cell patients.

in the body, called "iron overload." Too much iron can damage the heart, liver, and other important organs. Other problems may develop if the donor's blood does not match the patient's blood. "Mismatched" transfusions can result in a reaction that destroys a patient's red blood cells. This can lead to severe anemia and pain crises. The reaction may occur immediately, or up to several weeks later. Because of these possible problems, blood transfusions are given mainly to patients with a high risk for stroke or other complications.

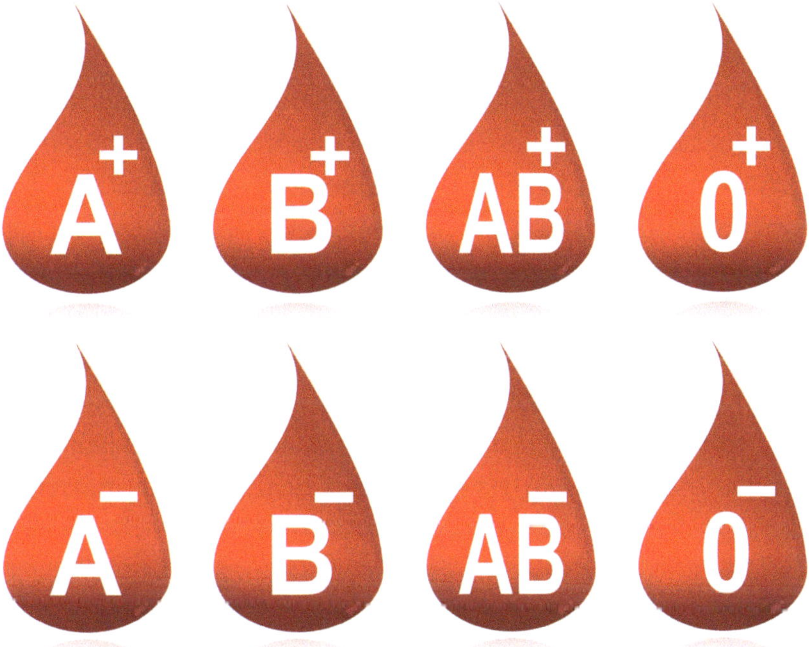

Blood types can be A, B, AB, or O. They can also be negative or positive.

THE PROMISE OF TRANSPLANTS

Blood transfusions do not cure sickle cell disease. They provide the patient with healthy red blood cells, but after a while these new cells die off. (Remember, red blood cells live for only four months.) Meanwhile, the patient's bone marrow is making new red blood cells that contain sickle cell genes. Bone marrow transplants replace the cells that make red blood cells with healthy new blood-making cells that do not contain the sickle cell gene. So marrow transplants can actually cure sickle cell anemia in some patients. However, like any procedure, bone marrow transplants do involve some risks.

Bone marrow contains a lot of stem cells. These are immature cells that have the potential of developing into blood cells (white blood cells, red blood cells, and platelets). In a bone marrow transplant, the patient's bone marrow is destroyed with high doses of powerful drugs or radiation. It is then replaced with healthy bone marrow.

HALF-MATCH TRANSPLANTS

Bone marrow transplants can cure patients of sickle cell anemia. However, the difficulty of finding a perfectly matching donor has meant that this procedure has not been available to most people with the disease. In 2012, a human trial conducted at Johns Hopkins University demonstrated that blood marrow cells that were just half of a genetic match could also be successfully transplanted. Dr. Robert Brodsky, Director of Hematology at Johns Hopkins and one of the authors of the study, believes that half-match transplants may one day offer a cure to 85–90 percent of sickle cell patients.[7] This breakthrough was selected as one of the Top 10 Clinical Research Achievements of 2012 by the Clinical Research Forum.

The best chance for a bone marrow match comes from a close family member, such as a brother or sister.

The transplant is not a surgical procedure. It is done in the patient's hospital room. The patient receives the marrow through a needle, just like a blood transfusion. The new marrow is carried by the bloodstream to the cavities of the large bones, where it settles down and begins to produce healthy new blood cells.

A promising new variation on this procedure is known as a chemotherapy-free stem cell transplant. This method of transplanting bone marrow does not destroy all the existing bone marrow using radiation. Part of the patient's immune defenses are allowed to survive, which reduces the body's chance of infection.[9]

The bone marrow for a transplant must be just as carefully matched to the patient's blood type as the blood for a transfusion. Otherwise, the body's own defenses, the immune system, could destroy the bone marrow.

The best chances of finding a bone marrow donor come from a close relative. Siblings have a 35 percent chance of being a match. The chances of getting a bone marrow match from an unrelated donor are not very likely. However, suitable matches may be found in various national and international bone marrow registries. These are lists of people who would be willing to donate bone marrow.

The procedure does not harm the donors. Only a portion of their bone marrow is removed, and their bodies soon replace it.

Chapter 5

Prevention and a Cure

In 2007, in the middle of a football game in Denver, Colorado, a healthy, 205-pound Pittsburgh Steelers safety named Ryan Clark felt an excruciating pain in his left side. He left the field and was taken to a hospital, where doctors found sickle-cell-related damage to his spleen. Clark had to have it removed along with this gallbladder. He lost thirty pounds after the operation.

Clark possesses the sickle cell trait, as do an estimated three players per team in the National Football League (NFL).[1] However, it had never stopped Clark from pursuing a successful career as a professional athlete until that day in the Mile-High City. Soon after he had recovered from his own ordeal, Clark and his wife, Yonka, faced another tragedy. In 2009 Clark's sister-in-law, Kim, died from complications from sickle cell disease at age twenty-seven. These experiences inspired Clark to establish

Ryan Clark of the Pittsburgh Steelers has sickle cell trait. He is unable to play football in places like Denver because of the high altitude.

> **SICKLE CELL TRAIT AND FOOTBALL**
>
> *The majority of people with sickle cell trait don't experience any symptoms or complications. However, since 2000, football student-athletes with the trait have collapsed and died more often than those with any other condition. As a cautionary measure, the NCAA Football Rules Committee of 2009–2010 recommended that student-athletes at its member colleges and universities be tested for sickle cell trait. In addition, coaches and trainers have been warned about the risks of intense training sessions and have been instructed to take certain precautions. These include: letting student-athletes with the trait set their own pace, build up their intensity slowly while training, drink plenty of water, rest between repetitions, and stop activity immediately if they experience any symptoms.*

the Cure League, an organization devoted to "tackling" sickle cell. The Cure League's mission is to educate people about sickle cell anemia and sickle cell trait, and to ensure that all patients have access to the care they need.

Although there is no widely available cure for sickle cell disease (other than bone-marrow transplants), there are things people can do to avoid serious health problems and reduce the number of pain crises that they experience.

NEWBORN SCREENING

In 1987 the National Institutes of Health (NIH) recommended that all newborns be screened for sickle cell disease, regardless of their race.[2] Even though sickle cell disease is most common among African Americans, this blood disorder occurs in almost all racial and ethnic

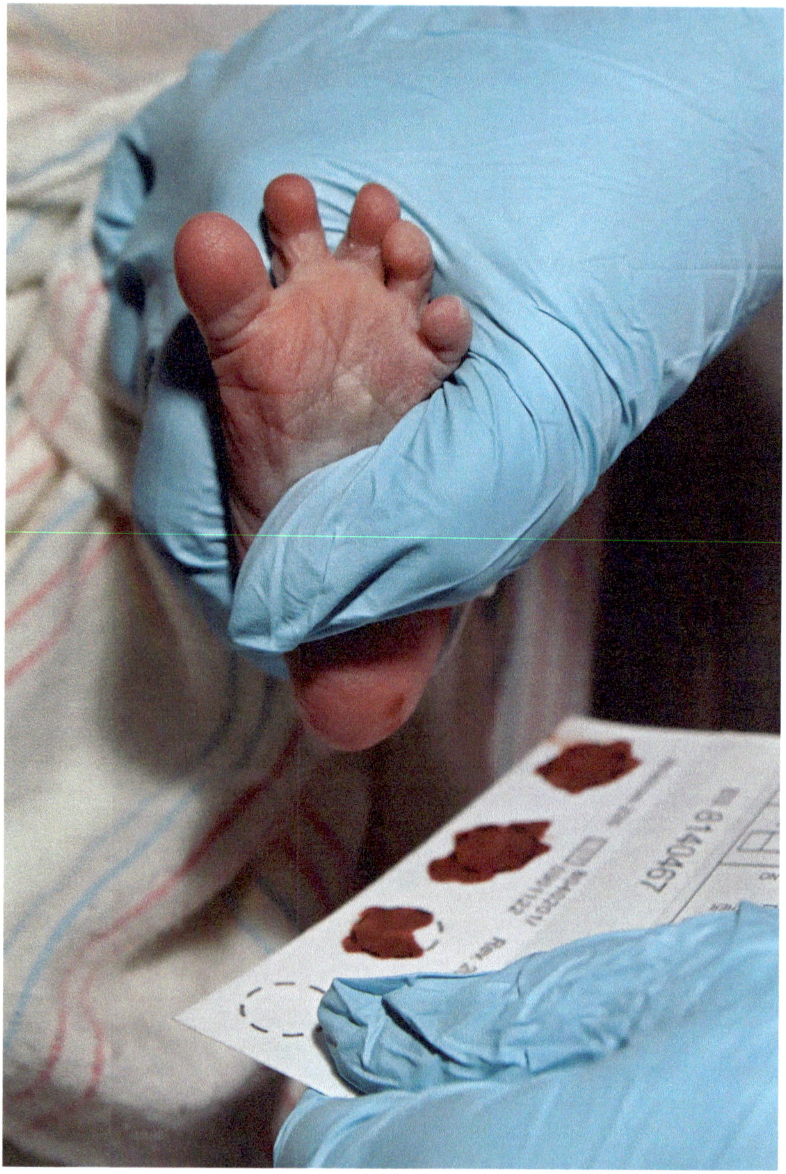

All newborns in the United States are screened for sickle cell disease with a blood test. The test is done with blood drawn from a heel prick.

groups. In addition, it is not always easy to determine people's race or ethnic group correctly. Skin color and other characteristics vary greatly. Going by typical African, Asian, or Hispanic last names can be misleading as well, especially for those who have changed their names through marriage. So, if only African Americans are screened for sickle cell, others with the disease will be missed. Therefore, everyone should be screened.

In 1987 the National Institutes of Health (NIH) recommended that all newborns be screened for sickle cell disease, regardless of their race.

Before the NIH's recommendations in 1987, fewer than fourteen states offered screening of newborns for sickle cell disease. Today, newborns are routinely screened for sickle cell anemia in all fifty states, the District of Columbia, Puerto Rico, and the U.S. Virgin Islands.

Sickle cell screening is performed along with the usual set of blood tests done on newborns. Screening has become highly specialized over the years. Computers can analyze a sample of blood for hundreds of different components. So the screening includes not only sickle cell testing, but also tests for a variety of hereditary conditions, including thalassemia and other hemoglobin disorders.

THE VALUE OF SCREENING

Over the years, people have questioned whether it is really necessary to screen for sickle cell anemia. There is no way of preventing the disease. However, studies have shown that newborn screening is very important in long-term survival. If a child is diagnosed with sickle cell disease at

People with sickle cell can no longer be discriminated against because of their disease. This means they can do things like fly a plane or join the military.

birth, daily doses of penicillin can be started right away. Infection is the most common cause of death in children with sickle cell anemia. Penicillin helps fight off the life-threatening infections before they develop.

Doctors recommend that penicillin be taken daily until the child is five years old, when the body's immune system is stronger. This treatment seems to really work. Studies have shown that babies given penicillin every day had 84 percent fewer infections—and none died.[3] Vaccination against common diseases, including influenza (the flu) and pneumococcal pneumonia, also help protect the child's health.

Identifying the sickle cell trait—not just the disease—is also very important. Usually the sickle cell trait does not cause any trouble for the carrier. However, under certain conditions—too much stress, overexhaustion from exercise or sports, or being in low-oxygen altitudes (such as climbing a mountain)—red blood cells may start to sickle, resulting in sickle cell symptoms. Knowing whether they have the trait can help people avoid those special conditions, where problems could develop.

WHAT IS GENETIC COUNSELING?

Many people do not know whether or not they carry the sickle cell trait. But knowing their status can help prevent sickle cell disease in future generations. Genetic counseling can help people learn more about the disease and the chances that their children will inherit their defective genes.

Genetic counseling usually involves a three-step process. First, the genetic counselor needs information on the family medical history. Are there any disorders in family

CONCERNS ABOUT SCREENING

Some people feel that genetic testing could lead to discrimination. People carrying genes that make them more likely to develop diseases such as sickle cell anemia or cancer might not be able to get health or life insurance, or they might not be allowed to take certain kinds of jobs. When sickle cell screening programs were first set up in the 1970s, these fears were quite realistic. People with sickle cell disease were not allowed to be airplane pilots, for example. Even some students carrying the sickle cell trait were forced to leave the air force military academy. Since there were no effective treatments for sickle cell disease at the time, screening offered no real benefits other than giving carriers information to decide on whether to have children. And because the trait was most common among African Americans, many people thought screening programs were racist.

The situation has changed greatly since then. Effective treatments for the disease make it desirable for people to know whether they carry sickle cell genes. Federal laws and regulations, such as the Americans with Disabilities Act (ADA) of 1990, provide some protection against discrimination in the workplace, and many states now have laws strictly regulating the use of genetic information for insurance and employment purposes.[4]

members? Second, genetic tests may be ordered if the couple has not yet been screened for sickle cell trait. After examining the test results, the counselor will try to calculate the risks of passing on the disease to the couple's future children. Finally, the counselor must explain to the couple exactly what kind of genetic risks they face, what the odds are, and what choices they can make to avoid giving birth to a child with sickle cell disease. If the couple decides to take the risks, the genetic counselor will prepare them for what they can expect: the treatments, the costs, the emotional stress involved, and the likeliness of success.

The genetic counselor also talks to the couple about other options, if they both have sickle cell genes and do not want to take the chance that their future children will inherit the disease. One possibility is artificial insemination, often used to help people who are unable to have children. This treatment involves inserting the sex cells from a male donor (without the sickle cell gene) into the female. Another option is choosing adoption.

PAIN PREVENTION

Although the disease itself cannot be prevented, there are a number of things people can do to avoid symptoms or lessen the number of crises. First of all, individuals with sickle cell anemia need to eat properly. Albert "Prodigy" Johnson, a Grammy-award–winning rapper with sickle cell anemia, says, "I try to stay away from poisonous food additives. I don't drink sodas or eat a lot of junk. . . . You gotta really eat healthy; break it down to a science and start learning how to read labels and know what ingredients are good and bad for you."[5]

ONE IN FOUR

If two carriers have children together, the chance of having a child with normal hemoglobin is 25 percent. The chance of having a child with sickle cell trait is 50 percent. And the chance of having a child with sickle cell disease is 25 percent.

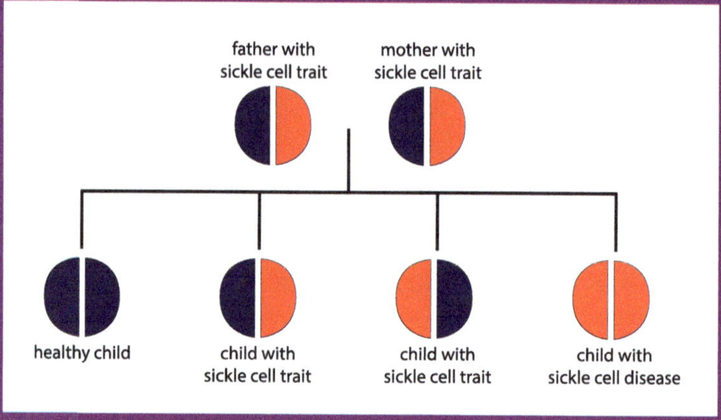

With a balanced diet—including meat, poultry, or fish; grains; dairy products; fruits; and vegetables—the body has a better chance of fighting off any infections. Taking vitamins in addition to well-balanced meals is also very helpful. For example, folic acid supplements help the body make more red blood cells. Folic acid (a B vitamin) can also be found in leafy vegetables, mushrooms, fruit, and liver.

Drinking plenty of fluids is also very important. It is a good idea to drink some water or juice every hour. This keeps the blood flowing well, which prevents the sickle cells in the blood vessels from clumping. When people with sickle cell anemia do not get enough fluids, they become weak, which can bring on a crisis.

A healthy diet is an important part of living well with sickle cell disease.

WELLNESS CHECKLIST

People who have sickle cell anemia should take care of themselves and see a doctor regularly. Here's a checklist of what to do to avoid problems:

- *Eat a healthy diet. Take a daily dose of folic acid to help the body make new red blood cells.*
- *Drink lots of water every day.*
- *Get plenty of sleep.*
- *See a doctor regularly for checkups and treatment.*
- *See a dentist regularly to prevent tooth decay and infections.*
- *Stay away from sick people.*
- *Learn about sickle cell disease and what signs of problems to look out for.*
- *Avoid overexertion (in exercise or sports), stress, and extremes of heat or cold.*
- *Avoid personal triggers.*

People with sickle cell anemia tire easily, so it is very important that they get plenty of rest. If they get tired in the middle of the afternoon, they should take a nap, even if only for a short time.

Although the disease itself cannot be prevented, there are a number of things people can do to avoid symptoms or lessen the number of crises.

People with sickle cell anemia should exercise every day—as long as it is not too strenuous. Just walking can help keep the body in shape and healthy enough to prevent illnesses. Exercising to the point of exhaustion is not a good idea, since stress can bring on a crisis. Taking a rest now and then can help to keep from overdoing it.

Cold weather can be very difficult for people with sickle cell anemia. One of the ways the body usually deals with cold is by narrowing the blood vessels in the skin. This cuts down the loss of body heat. However, the reduced blood flow means less oxygen in these tissues. As a result, sickled cells may develop and plug the narrowed vessels, bringing on a pain crisis. So people with sickle cell anemia need to dress as warmly as possible when it is cold outside.

People with sickle cell anemia should stay away from places where the oxygen is low, since lack of oxygen can cause blood cells to sickle. It would not be a good idea to go scuba diving or hiking in the mountains. Flying in commercial airplanes is safe because they are completely pressurized, keeping a normal amount of oxygen in the air. However, flying in some military planes can be dangerous because they may not be pressurized and the oxygen level may be low.

People with sickle cell disease should do some form of moderate exercise, such as walking, jumping rope, or riding a bike, every day.

It is very important to stay away from any kind of infection if possible. Since people with sickle cell anemia have a weakened immune system, even a simple cold may bring on a pain crisis. Pneumonia is one of the most common complications and is responsible for a large number of deaths of children with sickle cell anemia.

Most importantly, people need to know their own personal "triggers"—things that bring on their pain crises. Write them down if necessary. Figuring out what can trigger a crisis, such as colds, swimming in a cool pool or the ocean, playing in the snow, or being stressed out or exhausted, can help people avoid what is making them sick.

6 Chapter

The Future of Sickle Cell Research

Most advances in the treatment of sickle cell disease could not have happened without the willingness of patients to participate in clinical trials and to volunteer for risky experimental procedures. Some, like Keone Penn, made medical history.

Throughout his childhood, Keone was in and out of hospitals because of his severe sickle cell disease. He had frequent pain crises, and at just five years old, he suffered a stroke. Keone had to receive regular blood transfusions to ease the pain. But eventually, even the blood transfusions were no longer helpful.

Doctors thought that Keone was a good candidate for a bone marrow transplant. They tested his half-sister, but her blood was not a good match to Keone's. Then they tried to find an unrelated bone marrow donor, but they were unsuccessful. Keone's doctor, Dr. Andrew Yeager, wanted to try a new approach—doing a transplant with cord blood from an unrelated donor. Cord blood transplants had been used to save many leukemia patients, but the procedure had never been tried for sickle cell disease.

Cord blood comes from the umbilical cord after childbirth. It is full of stem cells, immature cells that can become any kind of blood cell. Cord blood transplants do not have to be a perfect match to work, as in bone marrow transplants. This provides more options for people who cannot find marrow donors, as in Keone's case.

On December 11, 1998, twelve-year-old Keone Penn became the first person to receive a cord blood transplant from an unrelated donor to treat sickle cell disease.

Keone Penn gets a hug from a doctor after giving a speech about his recovery from sickle cell disease.

Recovery turned out to be a long and difficult process. Nine months after the transplant, the new immune system that had developed from the transplanted cord blood cells started to attack Keone's own body cells. This often happens in transplants: The transplanted cells identify the body cells as "foreign" and attack them as if they were an enemy. This reaction (known as graft-versus-host disease, or GVHD) caused inflammation (swelling) in Keone's liver and intestines. He was given strong drugs to prevent further damage to his body's organs.

One year after the transplant, Keone was declared cured of sickle cell disease. His cord blood cells were finally working properly. There were no signs of sickle cells in his body, and he no longer had pain crises. He did not need blood transfusions to protect him from stroke.[1] In 2004 Keone graduated from high school and entered culinary school to train as a chef. Tragically, this medical trailblazer died in 2013 at age twenty-seven—not from sickle cell disease but from the complications of an assault.

A VALUABLE RESOURCE

The cord blood that helps sickle cell anemia patients used to be just thrown away. Years ago, the placenta and umbilical cord that pass out of the mother's body after the birth of a baby were routinely treated as "medical waste"—garbage. Now doctors realize how valuable it is. A 2007 bill in the Georgia State Senate known as "Keone's Law" established a state commission to oversee a system of umbilical cord blood banks and seek grants for stem-cell research.

In cord blood transplants, the donor is not harmed in any way. Blood is taken from the umbilical cord and placenta right after birth. (The stem cells would break down

This cord blood bank in Germany stores umbilical cord blood so it can be used later to treat diseases such as sickle cell disease.

within twenty-four hours.) The blood is then frozen and stored until it is needed. The stem cells in cord blood do not react to "foreign" antigens because the immune system of a newborn baby is not fully developed yet. Patients who receive cord blood transplants are thus much less likely to develop graft-versus-host disease. Cord blood is also less likely to transmit infections than bone marrow from a donor who has been exposed to a variety of disease-causing germs. Another benefit is that the young stem cells have an enormous potential for growth and multiply quickly in the patient's bone marrow. In addition, only a few ounces of cord blood are needed for the transplant, whereas as much as a quart or more is needed for bone marrow transplants.

Scientists have conducted tests on lab mice to learn more about how to treat sickle cell disease.

ANIMAL RESEARCH

Working with experimental animals allows medical researchers to learn more about human diseases and develop new tests and treatments. However, animals do not normally suffer from sickle cell disease. In 1997 scientists successfully transferred human sickle cell genes to mice, producing a "mouse model" of the disease. There are two kinds of these special mice. One makes both sickle hemoglobin and fetal hemoglobin, and has mild symptoms. The other makes only sickle hemoglobin and has symptoms of severe sickle cell disease.

In 2007 researchers announced the first successful treatment of sickle cell anemia in experimental animals with a new technique using induced pluripotent stem cells, or iPs. The use of human embryonic stem cells in research has been controversial. However, the scientists used skin cells rather than cells from a human embryo to treat the disease.[2]

Thus, cord blood can be used to cure sickle cell disease. But it is not a treatment that can be used for everyone, because of the limited supply and the many risks involved.

Cord blood can be used to cure sickle cell disease. But it is not a treatment that can be used for everyone.

A STICKY PROBLEM

Over the years, many people have attempted to solve the mystery of what exactly makes the blood cells clump together to cause a sickle cell pain crisis. In 2004 scientists at the University of North Carolina identified a "sticky" protein on the surface of the sickle cells that causes them to stick to the walls of blood vessel.[3]

More recently, a research team at Brown University developed computer models that illustrated how different

FUNDING NEW DRUGS

The development of hydroxyurea has helped patients suffering from severe sickle cell. However, not everyone can tolerate this drug. Researchers continue to develop and test new drugs in the fight against sickle cell disease. Drug research and testing is expensive. In 2015 a Silicon Valley research company called Global Blood Therapeutics attracted $48 million in investments to put its experimental drug, GBT-440, into a first round of human clinical trials. An oral, once-a-day drug, GBT-440 aims to link up oxygen and hemoglobin. This long-term drug therapy is designed to coax red blood cells into a healthier shape.[4]

This researcher is working with stem cells to find new treatments for sickle cell disease and thalassemia.

types of red blood cells interact to cause a sickle cell crisis. The 2013 models showed that the rigid sickle cells alone don't cause blockages in blood vessels, as had been previously believed. Instead, they team up with softer, deformable red blood cells known as SS2 cells. Both sickle cells and SS2 have the "sticky" protein. Computer models showed that the SS2 cells were far more likely to stick to blood vessel walls, and then the sickle cells pile up behind them, like vehicles in a multi-car pileup.[5] Researchers hope that computer models like these can be used to evaluate drugs designed to treat sickle cell disease.

GENE THERAPY

Bone marrow or cord blood transplants can cure sickle cell disease: The patient no longer has to take medicine to prevent crises. But these treatments introduce "foreign" cells into the body, and they can lead to problems on their own. Researchers are working on a better way to cure sickle cell disease—changing the genes of the patient's own cells so that the blood will not sickle. Unlike transplants, this can be done without destroying the patient's own blood-forming cells first.

In 2001 researchers at Harvard Medical School and Massachusetts Institute of Technology (MIT) announced that they had used gene therapy to cure sickle cell disease in mice. First they removed some of the mice's bone marrow. They treated the bone marrow cells with a combination of fetal hemoglobin genes and genes from a virus to help carry them into the cells. Meanwhile, they destroyed the bone marrow of two groups of normal mice. They injected the gene-treated bone marrow into one group and the

A RESEARCHER'S CRUSADE

As a child growing up in Wisconsin, Betty Pace watched helplessly while a close friend went through one sickle cell crisis after another and finally died. At the time, around 1970, treatments were not very effective, and the life expectancy of people with sickle cell disease was only eighteen years. Betty decided to dedicate her life to finding a cure.

After completing her studies in medical school, Betty worked as a pediatrician and also did research on sickle cell disease. Gradually she devoted more and more of her time to research. In 2004 Popular Science *magazine named Betty Pace one of the "Brilliant 10" scientists in the United States.*[6] *From 2006 to 2008 she served as Chief Medical Officer of the National Sickle Cell Disease Association of America, and she edited a major textbook about sickle cell disease and genetic research.*

Dr. Pace is currently a Professor at the Georgia Health Science University. Her lab is working on several projects involving fetal hemoglobin. Although people normally stop making this form of hemoglobin at around six months of age, the gene for it still remains in their body cells. Dr. Pace's group is trying to find ways to turn the fetal hemoglobin gene back on in sickle cell anemia patients. They are also trying to develop gene therapy to prevent the change from producing fetal hemoglobin to making the adult form in people with sickle cell disease. Either approach would keep the blood from sickling and prevent crises.

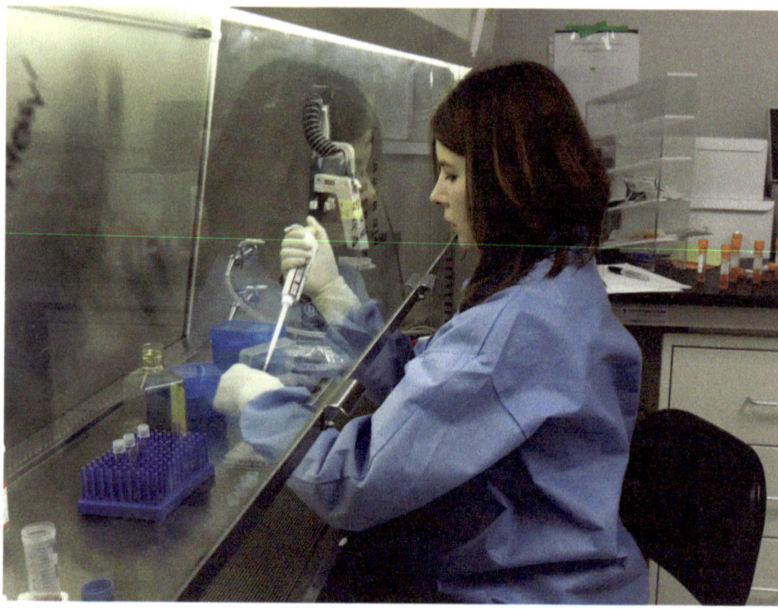

A researcher works with gene therapies, an area that holds a great deal of promise in the treatment of sickle cell disease.

untreated sickle-cell bone marrow into the other. The mice that received untreated sickle-cell bone marrow developed sickle cell disease, but those that received gene-treated bone marrow did not.[7]

In 2003 another group took the study one step further. Instead of giving the treated bone marrow cells to normal mice whose own marrow had been destroyed, they injected them into mice with sickle cell disease. The new bone marrow cells produced enough fetal hemoglobin to prevent sickle cell crises. (Just one thousand corrected bone marrow cells were enough to do the job. Remember, there are trillions of red blood cells in your body.)[8]

A decade after these advances, researchers at UCLA devised an approach that inserts a gene with anti-sickling properties into stem cells from a sickle cell patient's own blood. The anti-sickling stem cells are then infused back into the patient's bloodstream, where they migrate into the bone marrow.[9] There they begin to multiply, replacing the existing cells with healthy ones. Earlier test results with mice encouraged scientists to proceed with human clinical trials, to determine if this breakthrough in gene therapy might work for sickle cell patients. Clinical trials began in early 2014, and in October a research institute in Paris announced, "We are treating a sickle cell patient for the first time with gene therapy."[10] No one knows yet whether this revolutionary treatment will prove successful, but hopes are high.

GENE EDITING

Another approach in genetic therapy is a process called *gene editing*. Sickle cell disease is a good candidate for gene editing because the disorder is caused by a single genetic

Raising awareness of sickle cell disease is an important part of finding new treatments. In 2014 First Lady Michelle Obama visited with Courtney Davis, a patient with sickle cell disease, at St. Jude's Research Hospital.

mutation. That mutation could be edited out of a patient's DNA. Once the DNA is repaired, the cells would begin to create healthy copies of the gene.[11] However, altering genetic material can have unintended consequences, causing changes in the genes that have not been targeted. In 2002 a three-year-old boy undergoing gene therapy for an immune-deficiency disorder developed a form of leukemia. So scientists must proceed with great caution. However, with so many new advances in the research on sickle cell disease, it seems likely that better treatments and permanent cures will soon become available. People afflicted with sickle cell disease have good reason to feel hopeful about the future.

Early detection and better treatment help ensure that people with sickle cell disease, like these seven-year-old twins, live a long, productive, and relatively pain-free life.

Top 10 Questions and Answers

Is it called *sickle cell disease* or *sickle cell anemia*?
Both terms are used. One of the most common effects of this disease is anemia, a shortage of oxygen-carrying red blood cells.

Both of my parents have the sickle cell trait. Does that mean I am guaranteed to get sickle cell anemia?
Not necessarily. Having two parents with the sickle cell trait does not "guarantee" that you will get the disease. But it does increase your risk of getting it. Actually, there is a 25 percent chance that you will get it and a 25 percent chance that you won't have any sickle cell genes. But there is a 50 percent chance that you will get the trait, which can be passed down to your children.

If I don't have sickle cell anemia, do I really need to find out if I have the sickle cell trait?
If you want to have children, it would be a good idea. Then, if you marry someone who is also carrying the trait, you will know what you are facing and can make realistic plans for your family.

How do I find out if I have the sickle cell trait?
You take a blood test. This test will check for sickle hemoglobin and can also tell if you have genes for other hemoglobin disorders, such as thalassemia.

If I have sickle cell trait, does that mean I'm sick?

No. Usually sickle cell trait does not cause any health problems. But there may be some risk if you are in a situation where you are not getting enough oxygen—for example, if you climb a mountain or fly in an unpressurized airplane. Strenuous exercise in very hot weather could also be dangerous. Be sure to take breaks and drink a lot of fluids.

My little sister just got diagnosed with sickle cell anemia. Does that mean I have it, too?

Not necessarily—and if you haven't had any symptoms by now, it's likely that you don't have the disease. But there's a good chance that you do have sickle cell trait, so it would be a good idea to have a blood test.

When we found out that my little sister has sickle cell disease, the doctor said she has to take penicillin every day, even when she isn't sick. Is that good for her?

Yes, it may save her life! Children with sickle cell anemia can catch infections easily, especially pneumonia. Some have even died. Penicillin helps the body to fight germs before they have a chance to multiply and cause illness.

Can I catch sickle cell anemia from a friend who has it?

No, it is a hereditary disease and is not caused by germs. But if you have a cold or flu, it would not be a good idea to visit until you are all better. Your friend could catch the germs from you, and infections can set off a painful sickle cell crisis.

Can someone with sickle cell disease lead a normal life?

Living well with sickle cell disease can be challenging. However, the prognosis for patients with the disease has improved considerably in the last few decades. Patients are living longer and suffering fewer pain crises, thanks to drugs such as hydroxyurea. Healthy eating habits, moderate daily exercise, and staying hydrated can have a huge impact on how well a patient feels. Every sickle cell patient should be closely monitored by a doctor specializing in blood disorders. Following the doctor's recommendations can help them feel better and live longer.

Is there a cure for sickle cell disease?

Yes, bone marrow transplants have successfully cured sickle cell disease in some patients. So far, the necessity of finding a perfect donor match has limited their availability. Half-match transplants potentially may make a cure available to the majority of people living with sickle cell disease.

Timeline of Sickle Cell Disease

1910—Dr. James B. Herrick publishes the first medical report on sickle cell anemia.

1922—Dr. Verne Mason becomes the first to use the term *sickle cell anemia.*

1923—John Huck studies heredity's role in sickle cell anemia based on two families.

1933—Dr. Lemuel W. Diggs describes two forms of the disease: sickle cell anemia and sickle cell trait.

1945—Dr. Linus Pauling discovers that an abnormal form of hemoglobin is the cause of the sickling in sickle cell patients.

1956—Dr. Vernon Ingram discovers that the difference between normal and abnormal hemoglobin lies in a single amino acid.

1972—Congress passes the National Sickle Cell Anemia Control Act. It provides money from the government to fight sickle cell anemia.

1982—St. Jude's Children's Research Hospital in Memphis, Tennessee, becomes the first institution to cure sickle cell disease with a bone marrow transplant.

1983—September is named National Sickle Cell Awareness Month, the result of a 1983 resolution initiated by the Sickle Cell Disease Association of America and its member organizations.

1986—The National Heart and Lung Blood Institute reports that daily doses of penicillin are effective in preventing serious infections in children.

1987—The National Institutes of Health recommends widespread newborn screening for sickle cell anemia.

1998—The first unrelated donor cord blood transplant is performed for sickle cell anemia.

The Food and Drug Administration (FDA) approves hydroxyurea, the first drug used to prevent pain crises in adult patients with sickle cell anemia.

2001—Researchers correct sickle cell anemia in mice for the first time using gene therapy.

2002—The Health Resources and Services Administration Newborn Screening Program begins.

2003—Hydroxyurea therapy is found to improve the survival of adults most severely affected by the disease.

Sickle Cell Treatment Act signed into law by President George W. Bush.

2004—U.S. Postal Service issues Sickle Cell Awareness postage stamp.

2008—Newborn Screening Saves Lives Act of 2007 establishes grants for education and outreach on newborn screeing and follow-up care.

The General Assembly of the United Nations adopts a resolution officially recognizing sickle cell disease as a public health concern. Now World Sickle Cell Awareness Day is held each year in honor of that event.

An NIH panel recommends increased use of hydrourea treatment in adolescents and adults.

2009—Laboratory study concludes that modified blood adult stem-cell regimen reverses the effects of the disease in nine out of ten affected adults.

2012—Clinical trials demonstrate that half-match transplants may cure sickle cell disease.

2014—First sickle cell patient undergoes gene therapy.

Sickle Cell Treatment Reauthorization Act (H.R. 5124) is introduced into the House of Representatives. A petition urging President Obama to recognize sickle cell disease as a national health priority and to support H.R. 5124 collects the required 100,000 signatures in one month.

Chapter Notes

Chapter 1. Trouble in the Blood

1. Tameka L. Hicks, "T-Boz: Fighting Against the Odds," *USA Weekend Magazine*, November 7, 2004, http://www.usaweekend.com/04_issues/041107/041107t_boz.html.
2. National Heart, Lung, and Blood Institute, "Who Gets Sickle Cell Anemia?" September 2003, http:// www.nhlbi.nih.gov/health/dci/Diseases/Sca/SCA_ WhoIsAtRisk.html.

Chapter 2. The History of Sickle Cell Disease

1. Todd L. Savitt, "The First Two Sickle Cell Anemia Patients in the Medical Literature—A Study in Contrasts," *The Brody School of Medicine at East Carolina University*, Fall 1998, http://www.ecu.edu/medhum/newsletter/fall1998_p2.htm.

Chapter 3. Living with Sickle Cell

1. Centers for Disease Control, "Sickle Cell Disease: AJ Green's Story," *CDC Features*, January 22, 2012, http://www.cdc.gov/features/SickleCellDisease; and http://www.reviewjournal.com/life/r-jeneration/r-jeneration-las-vegas-teen-finds-solace-music-despite-pain-sickle-cell-disease.
2. National Heart, Lung, and Blood Institute, "Who Is at Risk for Sickle Cell Anemia?" September 2012, http://www.nhlbi.nih.gov/health/health-topics/topics/sca/atrisk.
3. National Institute of Neurological Disorders and Stroke, "Monthly Blood Transfusions Reduce Sickle Cell-Related Brain Injury in Children," Press Release, August 20, 2014, http://www.ninds.nih.gov/news_and_events/news_articles/pressrelease_sickle_cell_anemia_08202014.htm.

Chapter 4. Detecting and Treating the Disease

1. Adapted from Olive Downer, "Caring for Arianne," *BBC—Birmingham Your Community*, July 2004, http://www.bbc.co.uk/birmingham/your_community/2004/07/oscar/caring_for_arianne.shtml.
2. National Heart, Lung, and Blood Institute, "Reducing the Burden of Sickle Cell Disease," August 2011, http://www.nhlbi.nih.gov/news/spotlight/success/reducing-burden-sickle-cell-disease.
3. Arlene McKanic, "A Look at Sickle Cell Anemia," *AOL Black Voices, America Online*, 2005, http://bv. channel.aol.com/lifemain/health/sicklecell321.
4. Tracy Miller, "Man with Sickle Cell Disease…Celebrates 70th Birthday," *New York Daily News*, March 15, 2014, http://www.nydailynews.com/life-style/health/man-sickle-cell-disease-celebrates-70th-birthday-article-1.1723095.
5. Lab Tests Online, "Sickle Cell: The Test," *American Association for Clinical Chemistry*, modified November 15, 2001, http://www.labtestsonline.org/understanding/analytes/sickle/test.html.
6. Trisha E. Wong et al., "Update on the Use of Hydroxyurea Therapy in Sickle Cell Disease," *Blood Journal*, December 18, 2014, http://www.bloodjournal.org/content/124/26/3850?sso-checked=true.
8. Robert Brodsky, Web presentation from Johns Hopkins Medicine, April 18, 2013, https://www.youtube.com/watch?v=FnJjUKjt-Y0.
9. Johns Hopkins Medicine, "Sickle Cell Disease Research Among Top 10 Clinical Research Achievements of 2012," April 18, 2013, http://www.hopkinsmedicine.org/news/media/releases/sickle_cell_disease_research_among_top_10_clinical_research_achievements_of_2012.
7. University of Illinois Hospital and Health Sciences System,"Chemotherapy-free Stem Cell Transplant Shows Promise for Sickle Cell Disease," *Medical.net*, March 6, 2013, http://www.news-medical.net/news/20130306/

Chemotherapy-free-stem-cell-transplant-shows-promise-for-sickle-cell-disease.aspx.

Chapter 5. Prevention and a Cure

1. Chris Strauss, “Clark’s Sickle Cell Scare an Anomaly,” *Foxsports.com*, June 2, 2014, http://www.foxsports.com/nfl/story/pittsburgh-steelers-ryan-clark-sickle-cell-trait-scare-an-anomaly-010512.
2. National Institutes of Health, National Heart, Lung, and Blood Institute, “Sickle Cell Research for Treatment and Cure,” September 2002, http://www. nhlbi.nih.gov/resources/docs/scd30/scd30.pdf.
3. Doris L. Wethers, “Sickle Cell Disease in Childhood: Part I. Laboratory Diagnosis, Pathophysiology and Health Maintenance,” *American Family Physician*, September 1, 2000, http://www.aafp.org/ afp/20000901/1013.html.
4. Sickle Cell Information Center, Americans with Disabilities Act, accessed January 20, 2015, https://scinfo.org/world-wide-resources/americans-with-disabilities-actupdates.
5. Albert Johnson, “Prodigy: The Truth About Sickle Cell,” *Allhiphop.com*, February 4, 2008, http://allhiphop.com/2008/02/04/prodigy-the-truth-about-sickle-cell.

Chapter 6. The Future of Sickle Cell Research

1. Frederic Golden, “The Sickle Cell Kid,” *Time*, December 20, 1999, http://www.defiers.com/cordbld. html.
2. “Sickle Cell Disease: Model Behavior,” *UAB Magazine,* Fall 2009, <http://www.uab.edu/uabmagazine/breakthroughs/research/sickle-cell-disease.
3. “Sickle Cell Disease; Scientists Identify Sticky Protein in Sickle Cell Red Blood Cells,” *Blood Weekly*, November 4, 2004, 137.
4. Ron Leuty, *Silicon Valley Business Journal,* January 6, 2015 http://www.bizjournals.com/sanjose/news/2015/01/06/global-blood-therapeutics-sickle-cell-disease.html.

5. Brown University, "Computer models figure out sickle cell crisis," June 24, 2013, https://news.brown.edu/articles/2013/06/sicklecell.
6. Nicole Sweeney Etter, "The Crusade of Dr. Betty Pace," Marquette, Summer 2007, http://www.marquette.edu/magazine/fall07/crusade.shtml, and "Betty Pace, MD," Foundation for Sickle Cell Disease Research, Board of Directors, accessed January 20, 2015, http://fscdr.org/Pace.
7. Nathan Seppa, "Gene Therapy for Sickle-Cell Disease?" *Science News*, December 15, 2001, 372.
8. David M. Bodine, "Gene Therapy for Sickle Cell Disease Marches On," *Blood,* December 15, 2003, 4247.
9. Shaun Mason, "UCLA Stem Cell Gene Therapy for Sickle Cell Disease Advances Toward Clinical Trials," *UCLA Newsroom*, July 1, 2013, http://newsroom.ucla.edu/releases/ucla-stem-cell-gene-therapy-for-246937.
10. Sickle Cell Association of America, "First Sickle Cell Patient Undergoes Gene Therapy," October 14, 2014, http://www.sicklecelldisease.org/indexcfm?page=news&id=74.
11. Katharine Gammon, "Gene Therapy: Editorial Control," *Nature*, November 13, 2014, http://www.nature.com/nature/journal/v515/n7526_supp/full/515S11a.html.

GLOSSARY

acute chest syndrome—A lung-related complication of sickle cell anemia that can lower the levels of oxygen in the blood and be life-threatening. ACS is the leading cause of death for patients with sickle cell disease.

amino acids—The chemical building blocks of proteins.

anemia—A condition in which the number of red blood cells (or the amount of hemoglobin) is below normal and is not enough to support the body's oxygen needs.

antibiotic—A medicine such as penicillin that can destroy or inhibit the growth of microorganisms.

antibodies—Proteins produced by white blood cells that recognize and attack "foreign" chemicals, including those on the outer surface of bacteria, on cells that have been infected by viruses, and on cancer cells.

antigen—A chemical that stimulates antibody production.

artery—A blood vessel that carries blood away from the heart to any part of the body.

blood vessel—Tube that carries blood between the heart and all parts of the body.

bone marrow—Substance inside the cavities of bones that contains blood-forming cells.

capillary—A tiny, thin-walled blood vessel connecting an artery with a vein.

carrier—A person who is infected by a disease germ or has a gene for a hereditary disorder, but does not have any symptoms.

chromosomes—Structures inside each cell that contain the genes, coded in the form of DNA.

chronic—Lasting for years or possibly a lifetime.

circulatory system—The heart and the network of blood vessels (arteries, veins, and capillaries) that deliver blood to all parts of the body.

DNA (deoxyribonucleic acid)—The chemical of heredity, containing coded instructions for making body proteins.

dominant trait—A hereditary characteristic that is expressed even if the person has inherited the gene for it from only one parent.

electrophoresis—A technique for separating closely related chemicals according to how they move on a gel-coated slide or other surface in an electric field.

exchange transfusion—A procedure in which a patient's blood is slowly removed and replaced with fresh donor blood or plasma.

fetal hemoglobin—The main form of hemoglobin in the blood before birth and for a short time after birth.

folic acid—An important B vitamin needed for the production of red blood cells.

genes—Chemical units that determine hereditary traits passed on from one generation to the next.

gene therapy—The transfer of normal (or genetically modified) genes to correct a hereditary disorder.

genetic counseling—A program of testing, compiling family histories, and determining potential risks to help a couple make family planning decisions.

half-match transplant—A bone marrow transplant in which only half of the genetic material matches the patient's.

hand-foot syndrome—Painful redness and swelling of the hands and feet in children with sickle cell anemia.

hematologist—A doctor specializing in the diagnosis and treatment of blood diseases.

hemoglobin—A red pigment in red blood cells that carries oxygen or carbon dioxide. Its molecule is made up of protein chains (globins) and a central iron-containing substance, heme.

hydroxyurea—A drug that stimulates increased production of fetal hemoglobin, which can prevent sickling.

immune system—The body's disease-fighting system, which includes the white blood cells.

inflammation—Swelling, pain, heat, and redness in the tissues around a site of infection.

inherited—Passed on by genes from parents to children.

iron overload—The unhealthy accumulation of iron in the body, as a result of multiple blood transfusions.

jaundice—A yellowing of the skin and whites of the eyes; a sign of a blood or liver disorder.

malaria—A disease caused by a microscopic parasite, spread by mosquito bites. It is common in tropical regions of the world, such as much of Africa, the Mediterranean region, and the Caribbean.

recessive trait—A hereditary characteristic whose effects can be observed only if the person has inherited genes for it from both parents.

screening—Testing of large groups of people for a particular disease.

sickle cell—A red blood cell containing an abnormal form of hemoglobin, which changes to a crescent or sickle shape under low-oxygen conditions.

sickle cell crisis—An episode of intense pain that may require hospitalization.

sickle cell trait—The condition of carrying one gene for sickle cell disease. Usually people with the trait do not have any symptoms of illness.

sickling—The change of a red blood cell from its usual round, doughnut-like shape to a stiff crescent (sickle) shape.

stem cells—Immature cells that have the potential of developing into any type of cells or tissues.

stroke—Cutoff of the blood supply to a part of the brain, resulting in death of brain cells and loss of speech or other functions.

thalassemia—A blood disorder in which one of the types of hemoglobin chains is defective. Not enough hemoglobin is produced (resulting in anemia) and the unaffected chain builds up in excess in the blood.

thalassemia major—The most severe form of thalassemia; also called *Cooley's anemia.*

transplant—To perform a medical operation in which an organ or other part that has been removed from the body of one person is put into the body of another person.

vein—A blood vessel that carries blood toward the heart.

FOR MORE INFORMATION

American Sickle Cell Anemia Association
ascaa.org
Founded in 1971, the oldest sickle cell organization in the United States provides counseling and supportive services to families and individuals at risk for sickle cell disease.

Children's Sickle Cell Foundation
cscfkids.org
Dedicated to the well-being of children with sickle cell anemia and their families, CSCF partners with other organizations to raise awareness about the disease and provide support services.

Cooley's Anemia Foundation, Inc.
thalassemia.org
Serves people afflicted with various forms of thalassemia by funding medical research, supporting and advising patients, and educating medical professional and the public.

Sickle Cell Disease Association of America
sicklecelldisease.org
Dedicated to improving the quality of life, health, and services for individuals, families, and communities affected by sickle cell disease, while promoting the search for a cure.

Sickle Cell Information Center
scinfo.org
Provides sickle cell patient and professional education, news, research updates, and worldwide sickle cell resources.

Further Reading

Dudley, William. *Thinking Critically: Stem Cell Research.* San Diego: ReferencePoint Press, 2013.

Friedman, Lauri S. *Stem Cell Research.* Farmington Hills, Mich.: Gale Group, 2012.

Koramoa, John. *Sickle Cell Simply Explained.* Bloomington, Ind.: AuthorHouse UK Ltd., 2014. Google e-book.

Lambert, Marilyn. *Sickle Cell Disease: 109 Most Asked Questions—What You Need to Know.* Brisbane, Australia: Emereo Publishing, 2014.

Platt, Allan F., Jr., et al. *Hope and Destiny: The Patient's and Parent's Guide to Sickle Cell Disease and Sickle Cell Trait.* Third edition. Roscoe, Ill.: Hilton Publishing Company, 2011.

INDEX

A
acute chest syndrome, 42
air travel, 77
Americans with Disabilities Act (ADA), 72
amniocentesis, 55
anemia, 11, 38, 56, 60
animal research, 85
antibodies, antigens, 60
anti-sickling stem cells, 91
arteries., 35
artificial insemination, 73
awareness, education, 12, 15

B
blood cells
  averages, healthy, 56
  red, 12, 17, 21–23, 28–30, 35–36
  sickle, 36–38, 41, 86–88
  sickling reaction, 21–23, 36–38
  white, 35
blood circulation, 35–36
blood components, 32–36
blood tests, 52, 55
blood transfusions, 8, 50, 58–60
blood types, 60
bone marrow, 36
bone marrow transplants, 8, 62–64, 80, 84
Brodsky, Robert, 62

C
capillaries., 35, 36
carbon dioxide, 30, 32, 36
Castle, William B., 21
chemotherapy-free stem cell transplant, 64
chromosomes, 33
Clark, Ryan, 65–67
cold weather triggers, 77
Cooley, Thomas, 45
Cooley's anemia, 45
cord blood transplantation, 80–86
corionic villus sampling, 55
Cure League, 65–67

D
diagnosis, 23–25, 52–55. see also screening
diet, nutrition, 73–74
Diggs, Lemuel W., 21
discrimination, 72
DNA, 28–30
Downer, Arianne, 48–50
Downer, Olive, 48–50
drug funding, 86

E
electrophoresis, 52–55
exercise, 77

F
fever, 41
fluids, drinking, 74
folic acid, 74
football, 67

G
GBT-440, 86
gender differences, 50, 56
gene editing, 91–92
genes, 28–30

gene therapy, 88–91
genetic counseling, 71–73
graft-versus-host disease (GVHD), 82, 84
Green, AJ, 26–28
growth, underdeveloped, 42

H
half-match transplants, 62
hand-foot syndrome, 42
hemoglobin, 21, 23–25, 30, 45
hemoglobin (fetal), 53, 89, 91
hemoglobin A (Hb A), 30, 32
hemoglobin S (Hb S), 30, 32, 36–38, 52
heredity's role in causing, 19–21, 28–33, 74
Herrick, James, 17, 19
history, 16–25
hospital stays average, 50
Huck, John, 21
hydroxyurea, 53, 56–58, 86

I
immune system, 64, 82
induced pluripotent stem cells, 85
infections
  body's defenses, 35, 40
  FAQs, 95, 97
  overview, 8, 40–42
  prevention, 64, 74, 77–79
  screening, 55
  transmission, in cord blood, 84
  treatment, 71
Ingram, Vernon, 23–25
iron overload, 58–60
Irons, Ernest E., 17
iron supplements, 13

J
jaundice, 42
Johnson, Albert "Prodigy," 73
joints, painful, 42

K
Keone's Law, 82

L
life expectancy, 50, 65, 89
lung circulation, 35–36

M
malaria, 22
Mason, Verne, 19
Mitchell, Richard, 50

N
National Institutes of Health (NIH), 67–69
Noel, Walter Clement, 16–19

O
oxygen
  sickle cell disease, 7, 11, 21, 23, 30, 32, 35–36, 77
  thalassemia, 45

P
Pace, Betty, 89
pain crisis, 26–28, 38–41, 48–50, 58–60
pain prevention, 73–79
pathology, 21–23
Pauling, Linus, 21–23, 52
penicillin, 8, 69–71, 95
Penn, Keone, 80–82
plasma, 32–35
platelets, 35
pneumonia, 8, 41, 71, 77–79, 95
prevention, 8

R

Rise Above campaign, 12

S

screening
  amniocentesis, 55
  blood tests, 52, 55
  corionic villus sampling, 55
  genetic counseling, 71–73
  infections, 55
  of newborns, 67–69
  value of, 69–71
sickle cell anemia/disease
  causes, 32, 33
  epidemiology, 7, 13
  mouse model, 85
  outlook, 13–15
  overview, 7–8, 12–15
Sickle Cell Disease Association of America (SCDAA), 11
sickle cell trait, 21–23, 30–32, 65, 67, 71, 72
sickling reaction, 21–23, 36–38
Spates, Kier, 9, 12
spleen, 40
SS2 cells, 88
stem cells, 62, 64, 81, 84
sticky protein, 86–88
stroke, 41, 60
symptoms, 8, 9–13, 38–42, 48–50

T

thalassemia, 43–47
Totally T-Boz, 11
transmission, 7, 19
treatment
  blood transfusions, 8, 50, 58–60
  bone marrow transplants, 8, 62–64, 80, 84
  cord blood transplantation, 80–86
  electrophoresis, 52–55
  gene editing, 91–92
  gene therapy, 88–91
  hydroxyurea, 53, 56–58, 86
  induced pluripotent stem cells, 85
  overview, 8, 50
  pain medication, 11
  penicillin, 8, 69–71, 95
  vaccination, 71
triggers, avoiding, 73–79

U

umbilical cord, 82–86

V

veins., 35

W

Watkins, Chase, 11
Watkins, Tionne "T-Boz," 9–12
wellness checklist, 76
wounds, slow healing, 42